To Lukas, Doug, and Angela

With all my love

...and that the world may never be the same again

Copyright © 2010 Karen Murdock

2nd edition

All rights reserved. No part of this book may be reproduced mechanically, electronically, or by any other means, including photocopying, without written permission from the publisher. It is illegal to copy this book, post it to a website, or distribute it by any other means without permission from the publisher whether for free or for sale. However, feel free to send others to www.PlayingWithLukas.com to order their own copy.

Printed in the USA

ISBN 978-0-578-06028-6

Cover design by Derek Berghaus, www.derekbdesign.com

Editing by Andrea Susan Glass, www.WritersWay.com

Photography by Sharon Fibelkorn, Joan Malloch, Linda Walton, Hadi Khalil, and Robert Johnson

Contact information:

www.PlayingWithLukas.com

info@playingwithlukas.com

(714) 403-7730

Disclaimer: The information in this book is true and complete. This book is for entertainment and educational purposes only. The author and publisher hold no responsibility or liability for any information or methods presented herein.

Contents

Preface   Our Miraculous Moment 4

Chapter 1   Seeds 13

Chapter 2   Tragedy 21

Chapter 3   The Meeting 26

Chapter 4   Transitions 31

Chapter 5   Theory 37

Chapter 6   Principles 43

Chapter 7   Healing 49

Chapter 8   Exploration 59

Chapter 9   Reflection 65

Chapter 10   Renewal 69

What I Have Learned 75

Interviews with Karen 77

Press Releases 99

Frequently Asked Questions 105

Acknowledgments 107

Resources 109

Preface   Our Miraculous Moment

Where there is great love there are miracles.

~ Willa Cather

Lukas and I are in the round pen together twenty feet apart—our eyes locked on each other. The world has faded away and time has stopped. Nothing exists but our gaze. We wait knowing what's coming and sink deeper into the place where we go together, a realm where our minds intertwine, content in our union.

As I'm ready and raise my arms, a nicker filled with relief and joy erupts from Lukas and he rushes to me. At the last possible second, up he goes—a rear so full and majestic it never fails to take my breath away.

How much could one horse matter? I was about to find that out. This is the story of my horse Lukas...

"Karen, have you heard what's going on?" It was my web designer calling me. Strange, I thought, she's never called me before.

"No," I said. "I'm here at the stables with Lukas. Are you all right?" "All right?" she exclaimed. "Karen, the Associated Press story just broke, and the website is getting hits like crazy. I've never seen anything like it in my life!"

Over the next few months, we would see Lukas' story picked up by newspapers all over the world. This was followed by coverage on NBC, CBS, ABC, CNN, HLN, Pet Life Radio, RFD Radio, Equisearch, Equine VIP, and many non-affiliates along with multiple online sites and newsletters.

The media links on Lukas' website would stretch to many pages, and I would watch as Lukas' popularity grew across all age groups, horse breeds, disciplines, continents, and even species. His website visits exceeded one million hits in less than five months, and our Facebook friends swelled to over five thousand.

It started to sink in as the daily e-mails poured in, requests for interviews, articles and appearances became more numerous. Invitations to present my techniques at seminars and conferences began to arrive, and friends started to encourage me to record Lukas' journey.

Animal lovers are passionate about their pets, and Lukas demonstrated what they already knew about their own animals. They could point their skeptical friends to Lukas' website and tell them, "See what I mean!"

This would become a recurring theme in our lives. I'll give you a few examples. "Lukas is a poster boy for the potential of all horses, especially those facing bleak circumstances," wrote Kim Miller of *Riding Magazine*.

Animal Tracks added, "Is this horse smarter than a fifth grader?"

A poet in France, Francois Normandeau, sent a sonnet describing the effect that Lukas had on him: "...I feel humbled to be granted such company...As his grace and majesty are so imposing...A nobility granted by a valiant heart and a pure, vibrant, and thriving spirit...Knowing we only exist in this granted relationship for a sum of moments...Each moment a gift, cherished immensely."

"People used to say that Thoroughbreds were too 'flighty' to train. With a world-renowned trickster named Lukas to prove them wrong, who would dare say that again?" wrote Esther Marr of *The Blood Horse Magazine*.

Sharla Sanders, founder of The Second Race said, "What Karen has done with Lukas is truly remarkable. Often Thoroughbreds are thought of as 'throw aways'...Karen was able to take a horse long past the years when someone would think him 'useful' and allowed his personality and intelligence to shine...second chances are good for both human and equine souls."

Dr. Emily Weiss, the ASPCA's equine behavior expert said this in a telephone interview with ABC: "What is more amazing and more astonishing (than intelligence) is that this horse is so cued in, has such an incredible bond with its owner, such a great understanding of his human. The way they interact is pretty profound."

David Young and Leigh Shambo, at HEAL (Human Equine Alliances for Learning) requested to study Lukas and my techniques as a model for their therapy practice with trauma victims. This from Dr. Young: "I showed your videos to our class and read the words that you say to Lukas. You should have heard their ooohs and aaahs. I think they are now convinced that his horse-human connection is something way beyond training, but is about a very close relationship with sensitive two-way communication that has yet to be developed."

"Karen Murdock is proud of her horse and the tricks he's learned, all at liberty and without a whip in sight," said Lisa Kemp at the *Equine Chronicle*. "She hopes that his accomplishments can inspire other success stories. It's amazing what you can do with training methods based on kindness, patience, and a foundation of positive reinforcement."

Sharon Pucillo, a social worker wrote, "Lukas should be made an honorary social worker. His journey and his very being have positively impacted so many lives (both animal and human)."

According to the late Portuguese trainer, Joao Oliveira, "Your work is good, keep going."

This from equine photographer Sharon Fibelkorn: "We are all so busy today...so consumed by our own lives. So it's not surprising that I passed by the big Chestnut's stall daily while travelling to my own mare's stall in the barn and never really took the time to get to know much about my barn mates. Upon volunteering for the local Thoroughbred rescue in my area, I was reunited with Lukas and Karen for a photography day. I never knew that Lukas was an off-the-track Thoroughbred and the hot horse stigma that I had in my mind vanished. I knew Lukas to be very polite and kind, smart and funny. I knew Karen to be all those things too, and I am in awe at how one dedicated woman, whose love and kindness made a home for and a friend out of one fine horse. I am happy to call them both friends."

Dr. Paul McGreevy, recognized specialist in veterinary behavioral medicine at the University of Sydney wrote, "You have trained Lukas beautifully and deserve every credit for your patience, timing, and consistency."

During this time, I felt caught up in a swirling monumental shift and knew that my life could never be the same again. I was struggling to keep up with the flood of mail, life's demands, and a growing sense of the aching enormity of the situation. Countless new friends from all over the world expressed admiration and appreciation for what we had accomplished.

"I can't thank you enough for making my autistic son smile."

"Your message of hope gives our disabled students something to dream about."

"I've been depressed for a long time since losing my mother and miss the bond of animals. After seeing you and Lukas, I decided to go to the local shelter and adopt an unwanted dog."

"I run a small animal rescue in Texas. You and Lukas are our heroes."

"Thank you from the bottom of my heart for sharing Lukas. I'm a teacher and we talk about him in class as an example."

Lukas made it to the front pages of Yahoo! and Google as "The World's Smartest Horse" and then proceeded to fill those pages citing over one hundred thirty thousand references to him. Mim Rivas, who wrote the incredible story of the smartest horse in history in the book *Beautiful Jim Key*, also contacted us. "I know all about Lukas and am so inspired by your work and that we have a modern day example of what Dr. Key and Jim accomplished. The writer/director (of the movie) also knows about Lukas."

The World Records Academy recognized Lukas as "The World's Smartest Horse". The TV news magazine, Inside Edition, and Guinness World Records contacted us and Lukas was nominated for the 2010 Equine Vision Award sponsored by American Horse Publications and Pfizer. *Cavalia* stars Magali Delgado and Frédéric Pignon, in town for a show in Santa Monica, dropped in for a visit. I started to pay more attention.

Many people wrote beautifully about the emotional effect Lukas had on their lives and the possible far-reaching results.

Rosemary Neeb, Director of the California Thoroughbred Breeders Association sent this message: "Your hard work and unique talent, and a horse no one wanted, created the opportunity to accomplish great good. You and Lukas will help many people, help their horses, and bring knowledge and happiness to everyone who experiences your work with him. Your love for this horse is now measured by those who love you. God bless you."

Allison Evans, my first charge nurse when I was a twenty-four year old rookie, who I've kept in touch with for the last almost thirty years, had these encouraging words to say about my book manuscript: "Dear Karen, Thank you for sharing your inspirational story of your journey with Lukas. May God richly bless you as He knows your heart is for the benefit of His creatures. I too have seen your heart as you saw the big picture of saving and assisting the welfare of patients under your care above all. I truly wish you only the best as you continue in your path of teaching and aiding those who need guidance and love."

Oak Tree Racing Foundation agreed to fund a grant requested by the California Thoroughbred Breeders Association to film Lukas for an extraordinarily proactive project to insure second careers for racehorses leaving the track, thanks to Neeb's vision and dedication.

Through the efforts of Bonnie Adams, Lukas was appointed the "Spokeshorse" for CANTER, an association involved with rescuing horses off the track in the attempt to bypass the feedlots, where formerly proud athletes would be sold by the pound and transported across the border to slaughterhouses. According to

Adams, "Lukas is going to be what changes people's attitudes about how horses are viewed and treated, and his abilities will help people understand the changes that need to take place. He is our hope for the future well-being of horses."

As the economy continued to downturn, Adams felt it was necessary to form TROTT (Training Racehorses Off The Track) to handle the ever-increasing emergency "disappearing" calls, and Lukas and I joined her in her new mission. I felt driven by the chilling knowledge that if Lukas had raced during current conditions, he too would have disappeared across the border.

By this time, I was convinced that this book would need to be more than a training manual, which was my first intention, and I would tell our story from the beginning. I had seen that a horse could indeed make a difference in the world, and I've dedicated our work to sharing the happy results of "kind" training and to showing others that animals are intelligent and deserve humane treatment.

Chapter 1   Seeds

And the day came when the risk it took to remain tight in the bud was more painful than the risk it took to blossom.

~ Anais Nin

Being an intensely private person, I had originally, and naively, thought I could give you, the reader, a picture of Lukas' transformation by merely describing what we did together. It quickly became clear that his and my relationship is what has generated so much attention, and that our love for each other should be the basis for his tale. It's important for you to understand what formed my ideas and forged my beliefs to give you a complete picture of all that it took for this to happen.

I consider myself fortunate to have had the following experiences that have given me the opportunity to expand my perspective to include a depth and variety of experiences and emotions. This invaluable process allowed me to appreciate and develop Lukas' abilities in a very special and unusual way.

I was raised in Monterey, California. My father was stationed at Fort Ord Army base, and my mother worked as a key punch operator with the military. I grew up with three brothers, two older, Ernie and Bob, and one younger, John. My parents were second generation Americans from the terribly destitute Appalachian mountain coal mining towns. My mother had long harbored dreams of elegant parties, fancy friends, and fabulous trips. Instead, she had three children and bitterly reminded us daily of her sacrifices for us.

A former prisoner of war, my father had been taken captive at Corregidor and held for two years. He returned from battle with only eighty-nine pounds stretched on his 6'3" frame. A shell of a man from my every memory of him, his days (and nights) were filled with crying, shaking, and throwing up. His suffering and diagnosis of Parkinson's Disease when I was a baby prevented him from ever being a real parent.

My earliest memories are of trying to help ease the misery surrounding me. I had plenty of time for that pursuit as our upbringing didn't include rules or activities or any sort of structure whatsoever. We were essentially completely turned loose. I had my mind to myself...and the animals.

My greatest joy was spending time with our dogs outside. The time spent with them let me see another world, one of peace, happiness, and hope. I continuously watched them and played with them. My fascination with how they behaved and learned was insatiable. I would stay outside with them long past dark. No reason to go inside the house, and nobody ever looked for me.

And then **IT** happened—a rare family trip back to Virginia when I was five years old. Our destination was an uncle's farm. It was there I encountered what would consume the rest of my life—horses. From that meeting (an old mare with a droopy back), I wanted nothing else but to look at, talk about, study, and most of all have my very own horse. My aunt, a sympathetic soul, gave me a picture of Man O'War, a valiant racehorse. I would look at that picture every night before I fell asleep.

Not only did I not get a horse, I also never got a toy, any games, books, or other "frivolous" items. My mother "needed" a crocodile bag to carry in church instead. My wardrobe consisted of my brothers' cast offs right down to my shoes. As you can imagine, I became a prime target for teasing from other kids, and at the same time became very accustomed to being thought of and accepting myself as different. A girl wearing too large boy clothes, no usual accessories, or even having decent hygiene! I never had a purse or make-up, and my hair was cut at home.

Yet, I didn't really care all that much. I had the dogs, and I had discovered a new world: trick training. How many things could a dog do was my salvation. I also had a stable full of stick horses that I "rode" incessantly. During this time, I was developing what would become an indelible empathy for those in need and a deep and personal way of relating to misfits.

An incident when I was eight years old is etched in my mind. Our family went to visit my mother's cousin, his wife, and young daughter, Amelia. A year younger than me, Amelia not only had a bedroom, but a paradise! It was nothing like I had ever seen in my life: actual photos of herself and colorful pictures, lots of toys, books, even her own TV and radio. The most amazing thing of all was her jewelry box—full of trinkets!

She must have felt so sorry for me because she said, "Go ahead and pick something. I'll just get more." I couldn't even move. She held up a lovely locket and told me, "This would look so nice on you. Here, take it." I reached out and put the precious gift in my pocket, too shy to put it on in front of her.

On the drive back home, I showed my younger brother, John, my treasure. He, of course, waved it in the air for my parents to see. And my mother, who always drove, turned the car around so she could return the necklace, despite my protests that it had been given to me. My mother took me to the door and demanded that "I return what I had stolen because nobody would ever give me anything nice because I didn't deserve it." While I stood there at that door, I felt that I would burn in my own shame.

As you can imagine, I was painfully shy even before starting school. And as a four-year-old kindergartner, I would walk the half mile home to avoid it. But as the grades progressed, I had more and more problems with convention. The rules, boring assignments, and especially the other kids became increasingly intolerable. In junior high, I discovered that I could still pass the classes with very little attendance. I forged excuse notes from my parents and went through the grades with little notice.

I would much rather have been outside with my dogs and dreaming of horses. Luckily for me, one of our neighbors had a backyard horse. I spent endless hours watching him over the fence. His presence alone was enough to occupy me for hours on end.

By high school, I had decided that I wouldn't attend school at all. I couldn't bear the bus ride, nobody talking to me, and the complete isolation I felt. It's interesting to me now that the only time I've ever felt lonely is when I'm around people who shun me.

Truancy had already become a problem. You can only have cramps for so long. My parents up to now had previously ignored my now failing grades and warnings by school officials. They were barely able to manage their own lives, and they let us kids know at every opportunity what a burden they considered us to be.

The authorities were brought into the picture through the school due to my parents' lack of intervention. My mother let the principal know that "the police could have me." So, for the next six months, I lived in juvenile hall and assorted foster homes with increasing tension and problems. Here I was, a very young fourteen, too embarrassed to go to school, preferring the company of animals, now living with felons. I had no idea how to be in the world, no conception of conversation or interaction skills, entirely lost.

And so, not yet fifteen years old, I decided my chances were better if I struck out on my own. With nothing but a sleeping bag, I left this life behind, to create the life that was in my thoughts and dreams. For the next year, I would hitchhike my way across the U.S. Hostels, alleys, underpasses, and even worse were my new homes. I had no map, no money, and no itinerary—just hitching 'til the ride was over and looking for another.

Depending on traffic, the weather, and my mood, sometimes I would even go back in the same direction. The deep appreciation for my life and its incredible gifts was being cultivated—just a sandwich or a dry floor offered by a stranger would make my day. I could never bring myself to ask for anything and once lived for two weeks on a jar of peanut butter (and I was glad to have it). To this day, when I wake up and see a roof over my head, I'm struck with elation.

One time outside of Las Vegas, a trucker named Chuck Grant stopped for me. He was on his way east from a haul to Los Angeles and heading back home to Veyo, Utah. After talking for a while and asking my destination, he pulled out his phone and I heard him ask, "Honey, I've got a homeless girl with me. Can I bring her home?" As we pulled into the driveway, I saw my new family waiting for me...and a horse looking out from the barn.

Chapter 2   Tragedy

Although the world is full of suffering, it is full also of the overcoming of it.

~ Helen Keller

Chuck and his wife Connie had three children, and I spent the next year watching their children, looking after the house and animals, and of course, riding. Veyo is in a lovely mountainous area of Utah, and I spent every day exploring the entire countryside bareback and learning how to handle a horse. I did attempt high school once more in St. George, however, by now the difference between myself and others my age felt like the Grand Canyon.

I got a job in town, and at sixteen I met Dan, became pregnant, and married him when I was seventeen. When my daughter Angela was born, the rift with my family slowly mended as grandchildren tend to have that effect.

After I was married, I always had a horse. I learned how to train—Thoroughbreds being my first choice. They were plentiful, cheap, and came with an array of problems I found fun and challenging. During this time I read entire libraries of books, obtained my GED, and attended college while working nights as a waitress.

When I was twenty-two, a phone call in the middle of the night would forever change my life. It was my older brother Ernie, his strained voice making my blood feel like ice. "There's been a shooting," he said. "John (my younger brother) shot Mom and then killed himself."

Dan was out of town and unreachable (on a remote surveying job) and wouldn't reappear for several days. I threw some clothes in a suitcase and drove Angela and myself the seven hours it took to reach Monterey and what lay ahead of me. Nothing in my life could have prepared me for the death scene—no cleaning company would accept any amount of money for the gruesome job. Ernie, his wife Sharon, and I spent the next three days with our family members' scattered remnants in numb silence as we scrubbed.

The tears felt like they would never stop. My husband Dan, always emotionally distant, became even more so. He couldn't understand why I was so upset and essentially told me to just get over it.

Out of the depths of my grief grew my commitment to help other mentally ill people, since I had been unable to intercede to help my own loved ones. I became a Psychiatric Technician—and class valedictorian—in 1984 and began working in high acuity (lock-down) units.

Dan and I bought my dream ranch in Lake Matthews, a scenic horse community in Southern California. I started training horses professionally and also acquired Teddy, a 17.1 hand Thoroughbred gelding I had planned to keep and compete with. However, my already stressed marriage crumbled just shy of nineteen years when my father and Teddy died within two days of each other.

My choice and once again, I set out to find the life I knew awaited me. I had no money (our savings had gone into the ranch which didn't sell for over a year), just a rented apartment I couldn't afford (I held a part-time job at that time), and an eighteen-year-old daughter to support. I found a second job and a horse within the first week. Soon afterward, a "chance" meeting (a friend dragged me to a country western dance class), and there he was—my true love and life partner, Doug. We married within months of meeting.

I subsequently earned my Registered Nurse Degree (honors graduate) and continued to work in psychiatric hospitals during the day, while I trained my horses in my spare time.

My career in nursing has been entirely in acute care lock-down units—very intense, volatile, and unpredictable places that in retrospect helped me develop a much more patient, compassionate, and observant way of relating with others.

Over the years, on different units, I watched many small issues explode into huge crises—incidents that should have blown over, but ended up in unnecessary violence, injuries, and over-medicating with no benefit or improvement and often worsening the situation.

On the other hand, a few staff members were able to turn around even the most desperate situation almost single-handedly. Two nurses in particular, Allison Evans and Wanda Parks, took me under their wings and displayed the qualities I've most admired and have attempted to cultivate in myself: patience, appreciation, kindness, compassion, and humor.

Early on, I saw the important benefits of eliciting cooperation in a kind manner through fair and gentle methods. I also became more aware than ever of the effects of gestures, voice, body posture, eye contact, and attitude. Allowing choices, maintaining dignity, and promoting learning with positive outcomes—all these would become increasingly a part of my daily practice.

I owned several horses after Doug and I married—various breeds, yet always coming back to Thoroughbreds. They represent everything I admire: spirit, fortitude, sensitivity, and intelligence.

Besides their company, it was the training that obsessed me—how a particular behavior could be taught. This still drives me. I continue to read five to six books at a time on every subject imaginable to keep learning fresh and foremost in my mind.

After working with and finding a home for an especially difficult mare, I picked up the *Horsetrader* to find my next horse. Thumbing through the pages, I noticed a big nine-year-old chestnut gelding. The ad read: "Green project horse, 2K OBO." Worth a look, I thought.

Chapter 3   The Meeting

What is Real? asked the Rabbit one day.
Real isn't how you are made, said the Skin Horse.
It's a thing that happens to you when someone loves you for a long, long time,
not just to play with but REALLY loves you. Then you become Real.

~ The Velveteen Rabbit

Just Ask Mike was his racing name, California bred by Sharon and Ed Hudon, according to Sue Smith, his owner at the time. He'd had three races—two at Santa Anita and one at Del Mar—with back-of-the-pack finishes. A copy of his race records indicated that he "showed little" and ended up with two bowed front tendons. Only later would I find out that his lineage could be traced back to the great Man O'War.

After leaving the track and changing hands several times, he ended up with a family that had no previous horse experience. He subsequently became neglected and emaciated in a yard. According to Sue, "They didn't even know what he was supposed to eat, and his tail was a solid bat of mud and debris." Out of pity, she purchased Mike as an eight-year-old candidate for her amateur jumping program. After two years, he still wasn't fitting in, and so I came to meet him in October 2002.

I was immediately impressed with his large soft eyes and pensive demeanor. I asked to see him loose in the arena first, as I like to watch horses free—preferably not being chased around—to get an impression of them. I want to be able to soak in their natural disposition and tendencies. This speaks volumes to me about their personality and potential. Observing is as important as anything I actually do—carefully noting what's significant.

While he was being saddled, I observed from a point where I could see as much as possible to gauge him, paying very close attention to his eyes. He remained composed and alert while keeping his eyes on me—a good sign. Besides pertinent health information, I'm not usually too interested in hearing what people have to say about their sale horses as it has little relevance for me. The horse shows me just what I need to know, and Mike gave an exaggerated display of willingness to please—an eager nature and barely contained enthusiasm with an extremely gentle and kind presence.

His eyes, the deepest I've ever seen, never left me. The riding trial was brief and perfunctory—almost always a confirmation of what I've already felt. I didn't want to impose on the first ride or offend him.

Our lessons would take place privately in a manner designed to enjoy every second together without any time awareness, pressure, or distractions.

Doug and I went back to look at Mike once more the next day—my usual practice—and gave Sue her asking price. She agreed to deliver him the following day to the stables where I had been boarding for several years—a sprawling complex adjacent to miles of river trails. A very basic place, the managers had worked hard to create a family atmosphere.

The boarders, over the years, had taken over much of the maintenance, to keep costs down, and the overall attitude was cliquish and critical. Among this very talkative and casual group, I stood out like a sore thumb because of my shyness and unwillingness to gossip.

However, due to the management style, there was no outward antagonism. I was tolerated, which at least was better than some other places I'd been. Routine, as far as I was concerned. I had Mike.

When my new horse arrived the next morning, into his clean fresh stall he went. I would be the one to feed him small amounts and clean his stall during that first critical day. He would immediately begin to associate me with meeting his needs.

His stall would also occasionally be switched by me over the next few days. I would now become the new constant in his life. No requests, just me watching him and now, him starting to watch me intently as well.

I keep a low humming going much of the time to get horses to associate my sounds with certain emotional states. I hum during very relaxing moments such as when grooming or cleaning the stall to help the horse understand that I'm a calm and steady companion. This comes in handy when times get tense. It lends a reassuring reminder that all is well.

During this time of adjustment, I also introduced my voice and whistles to let Mike know that when he hears certain noises, food is coming. This makes for a very keen and seeking attitude. On the second day I went to visit him, he gave me a look too difficult to describe, and at that moment he became "Lukas."

At this time, I was working as a Nursing Coordinator for Canyon Ridge Hospital, a small free-standing psychiatric facility in Chino, California. My unit was an out patient transitional program designed to handle primarily two types of patients: those not quite ready to manage on their own after being an in-patient and those who were mentally ill but without the benefits or criteria to be admitted into the hospital. In this role, I determined whether or not the patient could be safely managed (because of their suicidal, homicidal, or grave disabilities) by me and my staff. I also helped to establish if they needed a subsequent higher level of care or additional services and when they reached a point that they could be appropriately discharged. It was a very intense and challenging position with a lot of patient contact, which I loved.

Due to my irregular hours, I did something I've never done before and will never do again: I enlisted the services of a local trainer to prepare Lukas for a career in competitive dressage. Dressage, a type of English riding, has always appealed to me because of its history, connection with the arts, and graceful movements. I found a trainer advertised (who will have to remain nameless) who seemed to have an understanding of what I wanted for Lukas. Things were soon going to go terribly wrong.

Chapter 4   Transitions

When the heart weeps for what it has lost,
the spirit laughs for what it has found.

~ Sufi Proverb

The time had come to move Lukas. The rental string (horses for rent by the hour) at the stables was unbearably sad to me. The owners fed the horses well and took good care of them, however, to see them come back lathered with sweat and limping from overriding (against the rules, but still done) was too much for me. Also, since the stables were so public, it was difficult to monitor visitors who walked over from the nearby park. I would find M&Ms, chips, and hot dogs on the ground outside of Lukas' stall that picnickers had tried to feed him.

I decided to move him to a show barn and arranged to help Lukas' trainer become established in the area. I offered to pay his horse's board in addition to his salary in hopes that he could pick up some business at our new stables. That wasn't to be. We moved to a bright and shiny barn, but Lukas started to unravel. He soon became unruly to the point of being unmanageable. He went into bucking spinning fits, he wouldn't stop running away, and he spooked violently at nothing at all.

As he worsened over several months, our relationship stymied and then disappeared altogether. The situation reached a dramatic riding showdown when the trainer wanted Lukas to turn (according to him), and Lukas objected and fell over a pole unseating the trainer. As if in slow motion, I watched in terror as Lukas ran wild and was caught and hit before I could reach him. Needless to say, I was sickened and thereby resolved to fire the trainer on the spot. He left the next day, and I elected to move Lukas yet again.

Our next barn was a very busy and serious place. Despite my careful inquiries and being assured by the owner that pleasure riders were welcome and numerous, I soon found out that was not the case. The only other boarder (non-lesson taking customer) was a gal that came at night, and I quickly found out why. The dressage trainer introduced herself (the one and only conversation I had with her in the almost two years I spent there) by asking, "You taking lessons?" When I replied that I only rode for pleasure, she sniffed and walked away.

Anne, the only one of her students who ever had the nerve to talk to me, explained it this way: trainers (all, not just at this facility) believe that I'm taking up a stall that could hold a paying student, and by making me feel unwelcome, they'd managed to drive other boarders away. This has always baffled me, because there are always plenty of empty stalls available for prospective students. Perhaps I'm old-fashioned, but I find this to be extremely rude. Also, according to Anne, it appeared that my training was too "fun" and that jealousy was an issue. So, I became the "woman who talked to her horse."

Once again, no matter to me. Lukas was my focus now. And I was having some serious doubts about being able to bring him back. By this time, he was a mess—sullen and aloof, reactive and resistant. Just approaching him was enough to startle and send him into the corner.

I set about getting his attention by pairing my voice and whistles with treats (small carrot slivers). I interacted a lot with him in his stall loose in this manner (just having him associate me with pleasant outcomes) to accustom him to shift his awareness to me. Also, since the shying had become so extreme, I trained him to lower his head to elicit a relaxation response that I could use when out of his stall if he became anxious. And I kept humming. Within a few weeks, he began to settle down in his stall. However, the most difficult challenges lay ahead.

His dangerous behavior outside of his stall persisted, but I understood that I had to build his trust in me. A journal entry I made during this period reads: "Lukas berserk when a dog ran by. It was all I could do to hold onto him." And there were many of these incidents. Nevertheless, I noticed a gradual improvement in his attitude over time, and he actually started to whinny when he heard me arrive at the stables.

His personality also started to emerge in small significant ways. He revealed a very sensitive and inquisitive nature in small bits and pieces. Lukas had his opinions, and he expected me to consider them. For example, he preferred certain areas to graze and walk, and if there was something that interested him he would insist on exploring it.

In the meantime, our riding work was perilous indeed. Not even breaking colts and salvaging auction horses (as I did in Lake Matthews) could have prepared me for what was in store. I've held onto a mane to remain in the saddle on exactly two horses, Lukas being one of them. I've never come off a horse in my life, but there were definitely some close calls during this period. I let his mane grow to have plenty of "grab," and I stayed away from any arenas where there were other riders. Because of his continuous bucking and spinning, I was always relieved to dismount voluntarily.

Well-meaning observers suggested to me numerous times that he (and I) would be better off if I sent him to the feedlot. I had even begun to wonder if he might be happier with another owner during this dark time. In desperation, I called a friend, Nancy Modgling, to see if she might be able to find him a good home if I were to give him to her. It was Nancy's encouragement and suggestion of a feed change from alfalfa hay to timothy hay that seemed to help flip the switch. His attitude significantly improved.

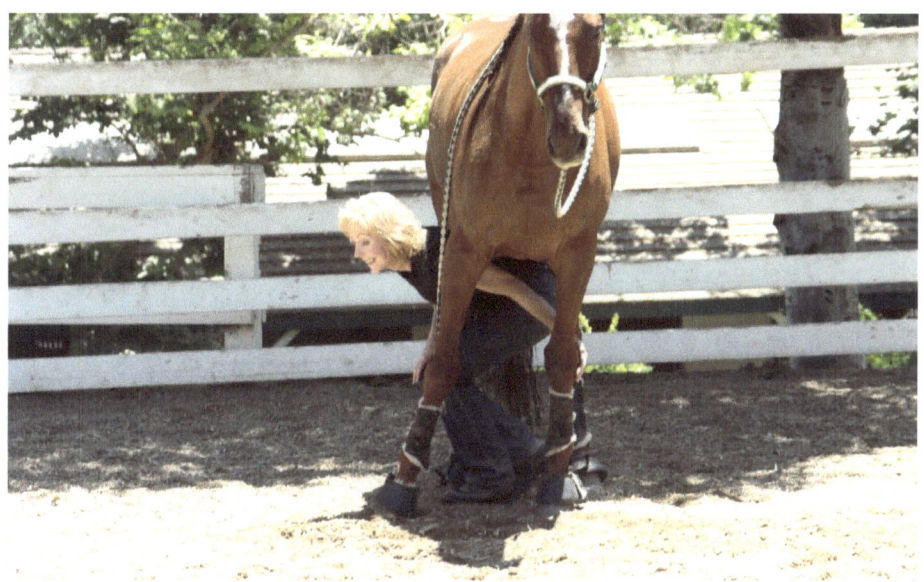

My plans for training Lukas certainly differed from the conventional methods. Under the prevailing systems, animals are seen as machines with little to no cognitive abilities, slaves to their instincts and without any reasoning capacities. Traditional techniques rely heavily on negative reinforcement and tightly prescribed regimens that seemed way too restrictive for us. I felt there was something missing in all of this.

A part inside me yearned for the feeling I'd had with my dogs so long ago. I set about to re-create that feeling without any agenda or goals, just the resolve to enjoy learning about each other and allow Lukas the opportunity to express himself. I now knew that I wouldn't give up on him the way I had been cast off. I was determined to find a way through.

Chapter 5   Theory

We rise to great heights by a winding staircase.

~ Francis Bacon

A way through. That was going to take everything I had, as it turned out. My three primary tools are **shaping** (the fancy behavior modification term is called successive approximation), a specialized version of **clicker training** (without the clicker), and lots of **positive reinforcement**. To start, I identify behaviors that I'll either create or capture and then use the tools to achieve that.

This system has the advantage of incorporating and complementing two major areas of learning: that which the animal does on its own and that which I can produce. By combining these two teaching styles, the effectiveness of the learning is magnified tremendously. Here's a closer look at this.

Without getting too technical, shaping is a process that uses a signal to elicit a response, the creating aspect I referred to earlier. I'll give a cue, starting with the subtlest message possible and wait a bit for some type of response. If nothing happens, I don't increase the pressure or intensity, rather, I'll wait another second or two. If there's still no response, I'll try a different spot on the horse, or an ever so slight vibration, or a removal and resumption of the same cue. This allows the animal to absorb and figure out what I'm asking for in a quiet and gentle manner. Doing less and getting more is the goal.

So often, I've seen an escalation of demands when all that was needed was some patience and a slight variation. Immediately upon any inclination toward the desired behavior, I simultaneously release the cue and reinforce with my voice, "Good boy" followed (usually) by a treat. Treats are an entire chapter by themselves, and I'll review that subject a little later.

So, now we've got a slight response toward our goal behavior with our shaper (light touch). I'll help you understand as we go forward how you can then expand and improve on that.

Next, let's examine how clicker training comes into play. Bear with me while I connect the two systems, because it will be the key to success for anyone training their animal. Clicker training is basically a click—in Lukas' case, my voice or a whistle—for a wanted behavior and nothing at all (ignoring) for the unwanted. I became fascinated with clicker training's effectiveness years ago, but didn't want to carry anything around or for there to be any delay to come between the desired response and the reward. As a result, I substituted the sounds I make for the click. In this way, I'm able to teach Lukas non-stop and avail myself of every opportunity for progress.

One other twist I added is the use of intermediary markers that inform the horse that they're going in the right direction (or not). A click is an all-or-nothing event. It either happens or it doesn't. What I noticed in my trials and errors were lots of lost opportunities to guide and speed the learning. So I made up a system based on the cold-hot game we played as children. Rather than a random erratic type of guessing by the horse, I lead him along by "hints" such as "yes" or "all right", the inflection lifting at the end as if to urge him on. Furthermore, if the animal starts to stray from the behavior I want, a simple "uh-uh" is enough to get him scrambling in another (wanted) direction, rather like a verbal compass.

Talk about fun! The lessons become an interactive playful game that results in the fastest, best retained, and eager learning I've ever observed. Moreover, I often add the markers—that encouraging "yes, come on"—at the tail end of a behavior I'm trying to teach, to stretch it out just a bit more to improve it. Now, for the treats.

"You're going to spoil that horse." If I've heard it once, I've heard it a thousand times. Treating has a specific purpose in my program, and that is to reinforce what I want so it becomes more likely to happen again. Additionally, I'll also pair up my verbal praise with the food rewards, so it becomes a secondary reward and can stand on its own if needed. It involves a carefully prescribed and detailed schedule.

In general, I tend to reward plentifully, especially at the beginning of a new behavior, then taper off to draw out more of an effort as the horse's understanding grows. That way I'm continually raising the bar, challenging the horse to offer a greater attempt to please me. To maintain that sort of eagerness, I'll change up the schedule from a fixed and steady supply of carrots to a variable—perhaps after every two or three good attempts—to finally a random incentive, for extra or prolonged attempts.

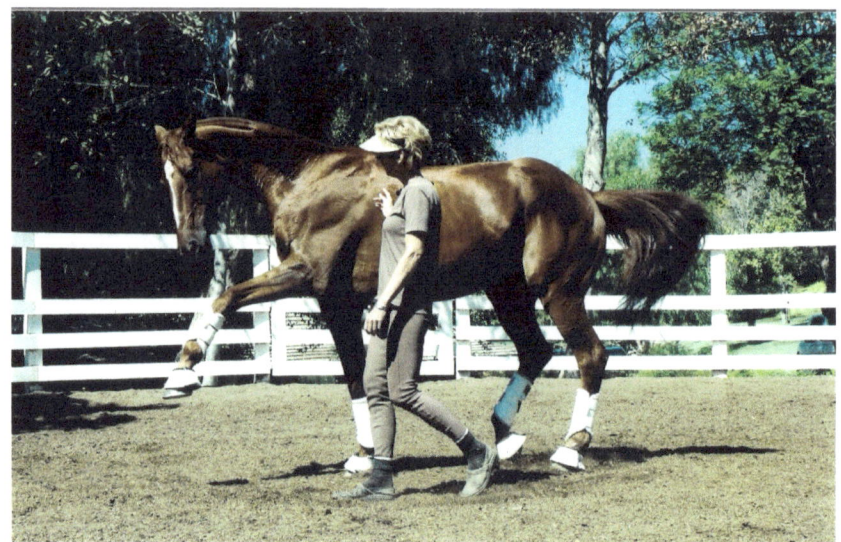

Also, jackpots—especially yummy treats or a large handful of the carrot slivers—have sometimes gotten us to the next level where no amount of cueing would've had the same impact or results. Keep in mind some important points when you're thinking about treats for your horse: instill manners and maintain safety. I never allow a horse to become pushy or demanding. Prevent bad behaviors from developing, because you'll spend at least twice as long fixing them. To demonstrate this, Lukas now holds a statue-like pose with a carrot inches from his eye while I count one...two......seven.........nine and (finally) three. Toddlers are even able to feed him his favorite muffin while he uses only his lips to gently scoop it from an extended hand.

So, I've covered the three main technical components of my system: shaping, clicker(less) training, and positive reinforcement. In the next chapters I'll start blending them to give you a better idea of how to apply them and when. I want to also cover a very important concept: that of **liberty training**.

Liberty training is done while the horse is free or loose, without any equipment. I should add that Lukas is never tied—even during hauling—so all of our time together is spent with him at liberty. For me, this is the best way to train. It's a way to help the horse figure out what I'm asking for. This type of learning proceeds very naturally, because movement becomes our communication and a bridge into each other's minds.

I've used it with all my horses, and it's invaluable to developing a relationship and understanding. It becomes like a dance that's flowing and mirror-like—art in motion without time or thinking, only each other. Lukas and I delve deep into this place as often as we can. It's our connection. I often feel that, through our games, Lukas and I have actually become part of each other.

Lastly, I must include a few words on attitude. A genuine sense of appreciation and enthusiasm go a long way in training—and in life. I always let the horse know when I'm pleased and can often be seen clapping and heard expressing pride in Lukas' efforts as he nickers in return. Heartfelt approval and encouragement are sensed by animals and can become almost a tangible bond linking us. Let's examine a few principles together.

Chapter 6   Principles

*The best and most beautiful things in this world cannot be seen
or even heard, but must be felt with the heart.*

~ Helen Keller

I almost skipped this chapter, worrying that it would be too technical or overwhelming for non-trainers. However, it contains information I hope will be useful in everyday life. You can choose what to apply in your own situation.

Most of my training takes place in the stall. I'm fortunate to have Lukas in a half covered twenty-four foot by thirty-six foot outdoor enclosure that I've had fully matted (however, we started in a twelve by twelve that also worked well).

Sessions are brief and enjoyable to avoid monotony and maintain his interest. From the moment I arrive at the stables, I'm training him every second that I'm there, even if only to sustain previous lessons. It may sound excessive or tiring, yet it's become a way of life for me—to pay attention, look for, and recognize the good and acknowledge an effort. This careful and appreciative practice has changed my outlook on everything. I can often be heard telling Lukas, "Let's pretend that didn't happen," as we move on to something that turns out much better.

I would compare it to artwork I've seen for sale at the swap meet (elaborately detailed depictions that contain pictures within pictures)—once you've seen the multiple images within the colors, you're then unable *not* to see them. I needn't focus on a stumbling block, and by averting a conflict, this usually results in another way of accomplishing the goal. Lukas didn't always absorb the lessons in a direct, linear manner. Often a lesson would go undone until a subsequent different lesson would help him make a connection. Interestingly, as Lukas learned to learn, the lessons would become easier for him, and I could often work on several tasks during one visit.

Even now if my mind wanders, Lukas will nudge me as if to enjoin me to return to the lesson at hand. I also try never to allow interruptions during our visits. It's not polite and painfully feels like a screeching, clumsy halt to me, and the momentum and closeness between us vanishes. The phone is off, and visitors understand the sign on Lukas' door very well: "I live in my own little world, but it's OK, they know me here."

Most of the training inquiries I receive have to do with the rear, bow, and lie down, and I always defer on these, instead emphasizing the need for a proper foundation and correct basics. What I've attempted to convey here is that when your training is correct, the tricks are only a by-product and happen in an almost effortless, uncalculated way. The tricks have never been and will never be my goal. They're merely ways for Lukas and I to interact, bond, and blend our minds—a bridge into each other's thoughts and tendencies. The tricks have also served as an educational example for people to see the possibilities of non-force training and give them the opportunity to consider another way of relating with animals.

It's important that you expect that the horse will want to please you and offer behaviors that you're teaching him. Definitely NOT a good idea to introduce some tricks early on in this process. The usual recommended order is face and neck tricks first.

Although I prefer to proceed in an unstructured spontaneous way depending on what the horse shows me, I would strongly suggest you follow the schedule in my soon-to-be-released training manual to increase the likelihood of safe fun and success.

Building on your relationship based on trust, patience, and mutual enjoyment will get you much farther than insisting on complicated maneuvers that the horse isn't yet ready for and may do damage that you'll have to address later on.

I'm often asked about punishment. In my opinion and experience, punishment almost always results in unpredictable, volatile, and ineffective results. I much prefer preventing problems to fixing them and will go to great lengths to replace an undesirable behavior with one I prefer. I've found this to be a usually permanent solution I can rely on rather than escalating negative punishers.

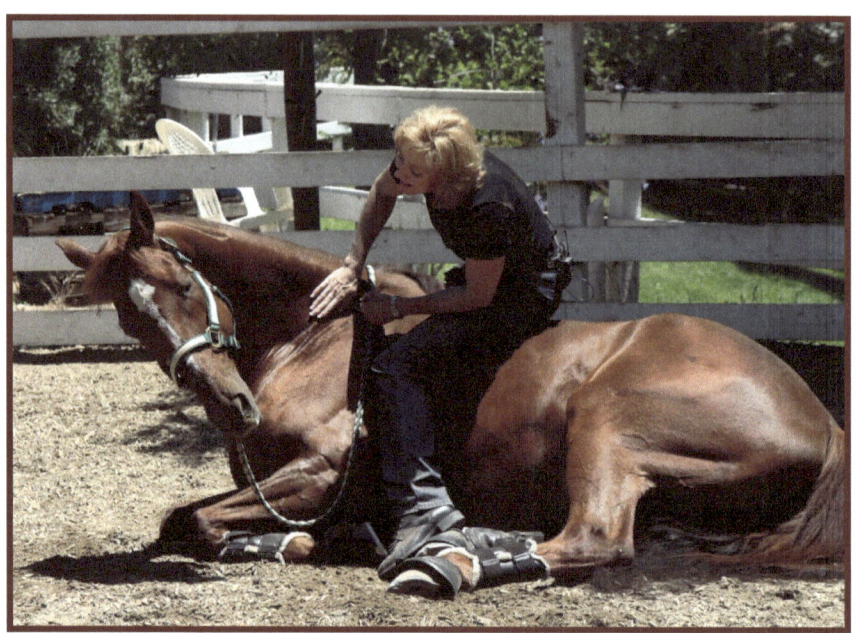

That's not to say that I don't set firm limits and have definite parameters for acceptable behavior. Lukas and I "cuddle" a lot and I allow him more liberties than I probably would ever extend to another horse. However, this comes from an established mutual respect and confidence. In the beginning and with all other horses, there are space requirements and always continue to be rules that mustn't be broken (biting, kicking and pushiness). As with setting limits for my mentally ill patients, rules help determine boundaries, and provide reassurance and stability for them.

"Your way takes so much time, Karen," is something I've heard more than once. Yet these same critics will spend *years* hitting or drugging the same horse to clip or load it! Amazing to me. An example here will illustrate my point. I was informed when I purchased Lukas that, "You'll never be able to clip his ears."

He now allows me to clip him fully without any halter/restraint whatsoever (including his ears, of course). "Impossible," you might say. All it took was hand grazing him while I touched his ears with my hands, a crinkly plastic bag, and then portable clippers (first turned off and then turned on) over a period of several weeks.

It's also essential to me that Lukas is not used for any type of disrespectful displays. I have to believe that his performing a movement/task is for a greater good and will leave a lasting and memorable impression toward our purpose: showing a mutually enjoyable, harmonious, and productive relationship. Casual or off-handed showing off is not a part of our conduct.

One of our important roles, as I see it, is including children in our journey. As a nurse, I've repeatedly witnessed the aftermath of trauma and detachment from nature. I believe an important part of this adventure has been to involve and entertain children.

It's for this reason that Lukas wears boas. Yes, I said boas, and feather ones at that! All holidays are celebrated with an outfit (our Facebook friends can attest to this!). His nickering and hamming it up for the camera are well known. As long as he enjoys his costumes, I will continue the tradition.

A final formal word on principles here. The cues I use are my voice (including whistles), body position, and gestures. I touch Lukas a lot—a gentle light caress, not a pat, and we're almost always in contact. Consistent and patient repetition—not drilling by any means, but a sympathetic guiding—is a mainstay and will yield the best results. It's not the techniques as much as the attitude and approach that are most important, not so much what you do but how you do it.

Chapter 7   Healing

Faith dares the soul to go farther than it can see.

~ William Clarke

I decided to teach Lukas the smile—his first trick. I was only hoping to find something he enjoyed doing that I could reward, because it sure wasn't happening anywhere else. When I went into his stall, he still eyed me warily, not quite ready to approach me even then. A low whistle, treat, and calm hello. "It's all right buddy, we're going to have fun."

For this trick, we'll use shaping and your "click." A light touch on his muzzle, almost a tickle, and there it was—a wiggle of his lip. "Good," (your "click" a secondary reinforcer) I say. (I use single words initially, simpler and more easily and quickly understood by the horse initially) and a treat (primary reinforcer). An important tip for this and future training: the reinforcer (secondary—in this case "Good") must occur at the exact moment of maximum effort/performance. So, when Lukas' lip lifted as much as he was able (given his learning *at that time*), at that utmost position, I marked it simultaneously with "Good." Rather than his getting reinforced many seconds later and when finished, the connection with his attempt and the reinforcement is strengthened.

With that, I stopped and did something else while telling him, "You are so smart." And I repeated the lesson a couple more times being sure to let him know how well he had done. Then I waited for increasingly larger smiles before treating. When the horse doesn't get the expected reward, he'll try different things, so just linger for a bit until you can reward him for a greater effort. Maintain your original cue position and pressure throughout the lessons, and keep things brief fun, and interesting. In two days, Lukas' smile was done.

A suggestion here: the best training and results happen when it's mutually fun for both the trainer and trainee. When I obtain a good response to a lesson, I'll stop for a break and sometimes even for the entire day. The learning will continue in the animal's mind, and the next session almost always takes up where I left off. In this way, the behaviors build upon themselves in a steady, pleasant way.

Now, depending on how far you want to take it—and here's the beauty of this system—you can make your cues as subtle as you have the time, inclination, or imagination to do. Lukas will now smile when I cue him from ten feet away. To fade—or eliminate—the tactile cue gradually, reduce it until it's absent. You may have to touch and take your finger away a few times before the horse figures out that your finger held up is the signal.

Be consistent in your hands, finger, and body position, especially if you plan to layer behaviors. For instance, because Lukas now knows so many different things, often there's just an inch difference in my requests. Personally, I fade every tactile cue. Lukas will do whatever I ask from my body position, gestures, movements, and whistles. I happen to feel that it demonstrates an extreme example of what can be accomplished without the use of force, and it shows others the wonderful possibilities. However, you can have tons of fun leaving it as a touching trick. This is meant to spark a fresh and interesting way to relate to your horse. Rules—except for safety—in this case can be flexible.

You might be wondering why I haven't said anything about verbal cues. I don't use verbal cues per se except with some of the cognitive tasks that Lukas now does. I find it bothersome and distracting, and I much prefer the intricate, intimate allure of slight, delicate exchanges. That's not to say you shouldn't use them if that's your style.

If there's one thing you get from this book, please understand that this is only meant as a guide and reference. The whole point is to have an enjoyable relationship with your horse, whether it's talking, touching, pointing, or laughing. Remember that almost all the information contained in this book came from my mind. I do hope years from now to see all sorts of creative and joyful effects from sharing my experiences with Lukas.

"What if the horse starts doing things on his own?" I'm often asked. Not to be vague, but this is very discretionary, and I won't tell you one way or the other except to offer some guidelines. If an animal is repetitively performing a behavior, and it's not something I want to perpetuate, I either ignore it or use distraction, simple as that. No attention, words, nothing, or we go on to something else. However, and this is a big however, I will be very aware of any behaviors I might want to keep or use.

For instance, when I taught Lukas to wave, he would wave continuously. "That's just begging," I told him and went about my chores. On one particular occasion, I happened to step behind him, and he turned as well, still waving. Thus his jambet (180° three-legged pivot) was born—an example of a "captured" moment. So the lesson here is to be open and ready to look for the good and try to dismiss what you don't want or doesn't work.

After the smile, I wanted to incorporate more moving tricks to help Lukas learn to control his body and also so he would allow me to move him in different ways. For this, I selected the Spanish Walk, my all-time favorite movement. So much so that I've also taught it to Wendel, my Cavalier therapy dog. For this maneuver, the animal performs an exaggerated lifting of the front legs only. It's a graceful, swinging display that I've always thought looked spectacular.

Lukas, however, thought I'd lost my mind. I should mention here that I don't use or even own a whip, once again to demonstrate that horses can learn without the use of force. Everything that Lukas knows and does has been taught with kindness and patience.

I would apply the cue, and he'd try to move over or back up, a quizzical look on his face. An easy fix for this is to attempt these early lessons in a corner of the stall. "It's all right," I'd tell him, "just a tiny move is all I want." The cue in Lukas' case started with my foot touching the side of his ankle. (If this doesn't get a response, you can try other areas of his legs/body). This is another example of shaping, as you'll recall, applying a cue and getting an inclination in the desired direction. Remember to use your "click" at the maximum moment to mark it for better understanding by the horse. Over the next several weeks, as I moved the cue up to his shoulder ("transferring"), he was able to lift each leg separately, as I switched sides and cued each side individually.

When I can get a reliable response in the stall, I take it outside. I want the horse to learn to deal with distractions thereby solidifying the lessons. Rather than disappointment over a feeble or unsatisfactory response or lesson, I make mental notes about areas needing work or attention. I consider all issues an opportunity to learn and improve.

By now, I had removed the touch cue for leg lifts, replacing it with a slight upward pull on the lead line (which I dispense with as soon as possible), and the sound I reserve for Spanish Walk only (as in tsk, tsk). From there, I coordinated this request with a step forward and—voila! —in two weeks we had it. It wasn't all eureka moments in those first few months. The bow (a dramatic movement where the horse rests a foreleg on the ground and lowers his body close to the ground) was stalled and wouldn't progress for weeks. Turns out Lukas only needed some time to adjust his balance and comfort level and has never had trouble with it since.

Allow me to interject a "captured" example here for you to think about before we go on. Liberty is the most powerful influence I have. With it I can mold and create what I want and strip away the impediments in a soft and gentle way. It's similar to a potter's wheel with small adjustments and a flowingness to it. The trick training I do is unlike what has been traditionally practiced. Typically most trick trainers will use pins to prick areas, ammonia for the smile, and ropes, chains, and whips to achieve their goals. I find this detestable. My system uses none of that and instead relies on my techniques and awareness of the horse.

That said, let's consider the **lay down**. The trick training books I've seen have you running a long line under the horse, over the saddle, from the leg, etc. All I did was put Lukas in a sandy pen after a short workout and cue him. I faced him at an angle, blocked his shoulder with my shoulder somewhat, and cued by pointing to the ground. Following that, I generalized the cue to other areas and made sure I always carried his favorite muffins with me for this one. I then used my marker signal to draw out his lay down so he would remain there. That way, I captured something he offered on his own—I wasn't going to force him down—and reinforced it lavishly (at first).

An important word about the release: for every cue/request and the animal's response, it's important to follow up with a release as well. This signals an end to the trick/maneuver, and it becomes understood that until the release signal is given, the behavior continues. My own cessation signal for Lukas is a short sharp whistle. Think of it as the recess bell; until he hears that he must continue his work. For instance, if I ask for him to Spanish Walk around me, that's one signal (a flick of my wrist and a drawn out whistle). I can also offer intermediary signals ("yes", "come on", and the repeated drawn out whistle) if he lags, and finally the release (stop) signal.

This keeps the horse from discontinuing the behavior on his own. In the case of the lay down, for instance, initially of course Lukas would get up earlier than I wanted. I paired my cessation signal—the short sharp whistle—with his *first inclination* to rise so he would connect the two. Eventually, he began to wait for my whistle and now stays until he hears it.

I receive the most mail about spooking, that is, the horse shies or startles. People ask me what can be done about it. Lukas was one of the worst as far as this goes. He would spook in his own stall, and we couldn't walk five feet without him finding something to be alarmed at. Now, at the last event we went to (The Equine Affaire in Pomona, California), you name it and we saw it: balloons, strollers, umbrellas, carriages, vendor's row, all without even a second glance from him.

An example of a lesson might help here. One particular ride stands out in my memory, because my foot actually came out of the stirrup for the first time ever. It was an ordinary day. I noticed a few riders tacking up, and we were to have the arena to ourselves for a little while—always a good thing in those early days. The large arena had a few small jumps and a couple of barrels in it for students to practice with. Nothing different from my quick—and ever vigilant—scanning.

On this day, however, one of the barrels at the far end of the arena had turned over. That alone was enough to send Lukas bucking and spinning and me looking for my missing stirrup. To fix this, I got him under control and just circled where he was comfortable, gradually increasing the circle until we were riding right around it. I show the horse what I expect, give him something positive to work on, and don't make matters worse by punishing.

At the exact moment a horse orients to something—and you've seen it happen—the ears prick, the body stiffens, the nostrils start to flare, and that's our chance to break the cycle. *Before* that point is when I'll hum, perhaps add a circle (while leading or riding) if possible, provide a distraction (horses don't think about more than one thing at a time), all the while maintaining a nonchalant attitude. I can also insist that the horse do something he's familiar with to give him a way to channel his energy and provide a comfortable and familiar task that's reassuring. I'm the horse's inner regulator, and I believe they do sense and mirror our feelings and expectations. By maintaining control of myself at all times, I'm thereby cultivating an unshakeable trust and confidence of them in me.

Change was tugging at me again. The hospital had recently fired the administrator and replaced her with an accountant. I was informed that my duties now consisted of strictly paperwork—no more patient interaction. Documenting on patients I couldn't talk to was not acceptable to me, so I resigned.

Over the years, I've had many, many jobs. I'll only stay in a position if it's beneficial to my patients. No amount of work bothers me, however, I must feel that what I do is meaningful. Also, there had been an accident with another horse at the stables that left a bad taste in my mouth. Coincidentally, my vet casually mentioned to me that Lukas would be very happy at an Equestrian Center that she knew about. After going to look at it and being thoroughly impressed, Lukas and I were on the move again.

Chapter 8   Exploration

You can't cross the sea merely by staring at the water.

~ Rabindranath Tagore

Brookside Equestrian Center was—and still is—one of the loveliest place I had ever seen in my life. Set on twenty-eight forested acres in the heart of Los Angeles County, it's a historical site and had been a set location for the movie "National Velvet". It's also a training facility for the U.S. Equestrian Team and attracts world renowned clinicians. The owners, Linda and Keith Walton, welcomed me as family, and I felt I'd found a second home.

At the time, three-day eventing—cross-country, stadium jumping, and dressage—was the focus of the barn clientele. Immediately upon meeting the eventing trainer and her assistant, I knew my presence was resented. In the almost two years I spent there, I experienced a very icy atmosphere around them.

A few of their students—Rhonda, Katie, and Nedra—were able to think for themselves and kept me from leaving in disgust. Of course, I never mentioned a word to the Waltons, who would have intervened. I've still not been able to bring myself to ask for a single thing from anyone. To this day, I don't have time for people who require money or "permission" to act civilly. While I'm on the subject, I'll just add that it still surprises me when indigent homeless patients without so much as a pillow, are able to muster more manners than most of the horse trainers I've encountered. Are we not all involved with animals out of care and concern for their welfare?

Lukas settled in like he'd been there his whole life. The winding wooded trails became a restorative haven for us, and we wandered in peaceful, happy contemplation. Our relationship was becoming close and comfortable. His antics had diminished to the point that his mane had now become ornamental rather than a life-saver. By this time, mid-2004, his tricks included the smile, Spanish Walk, nod, reverence (stretched out with his head between his front legs), pose, pedestal, and bow.

As it turns out, the bow, which had given us so much trouble earlier, was only a pattern of behavior that's quite normal for Lukas. It's similar to how children learn: when something new is presented, they need time to absorb it before using it with ease. I began to also notice something very intriguing about our interactions—Lukas wasn't just complying with my requests, he was actually anticipating and attempting to go further than I had planned during our sessions.

He had learned how to learn and wanted more. If I set aside his toys, he would reach for them. When I brought out his desk, he would nicker. "We played for hours and Lukas wanted to keep going. What a horse!" read one of my journal entries from those days. I began to wonder how to teach him all he wanted to learn.

It occurred to me to experiment with cognitive tasks out of my own curiosity. I've long questioned the prevailing belief that horses are dumb creatures. Current data on horse intelligence is based on results from tightly controlled labs using repetitive machine trials. This has been an important development to provide statistics and scientific validity. However, it went against all of my gut feelings. I wasn't able to learn in that type of environment. How could Lukas do so? In my opinion (and experience), the learning process is a social and interactive experience. I decided to teach him in a way that I would've liked to have been taught and what would've made sense to me. "Lukas, we're going to school....together," I told him.

First up was the touch, an indispensable ability for all our future games. For Lukas, not at all mouthy or inclined to explore with his lips, this would take a while. I started with my hand—a little treat in a loosely held fist—and we'd practice his following and contact. This also taught him a lot about distance and depth. Current experts claim that horses have a blind spot six to nine inches from their muzzle. Because of this, Lukas was able to teach himself to gauge how close or far something was. An added benefit was that his spookiness was now more controllable as he would listen to my request to touch something which overrode his fear reactions. His curiosity and play drive were expanding every day.

Since I wanted our first lesson to be with something soft (to avoid any negative mishaps), I chose his green towel. When he understood to touch it from my holding it, I then moved it to his "desk", a little fold-up picnic table with a non-skid surface glued on the top. For this, I told him to "Get the green towel," and boy, did he get it! "Lukas wouldn't leave his towel alone today. He found it wherever I put it!," I wrote in a journal entry during this time. This led to color discrimination, fetching, catching, and hide and seek. What could I teach him next, I wondered. A trip to the hardware store gave me my answer.

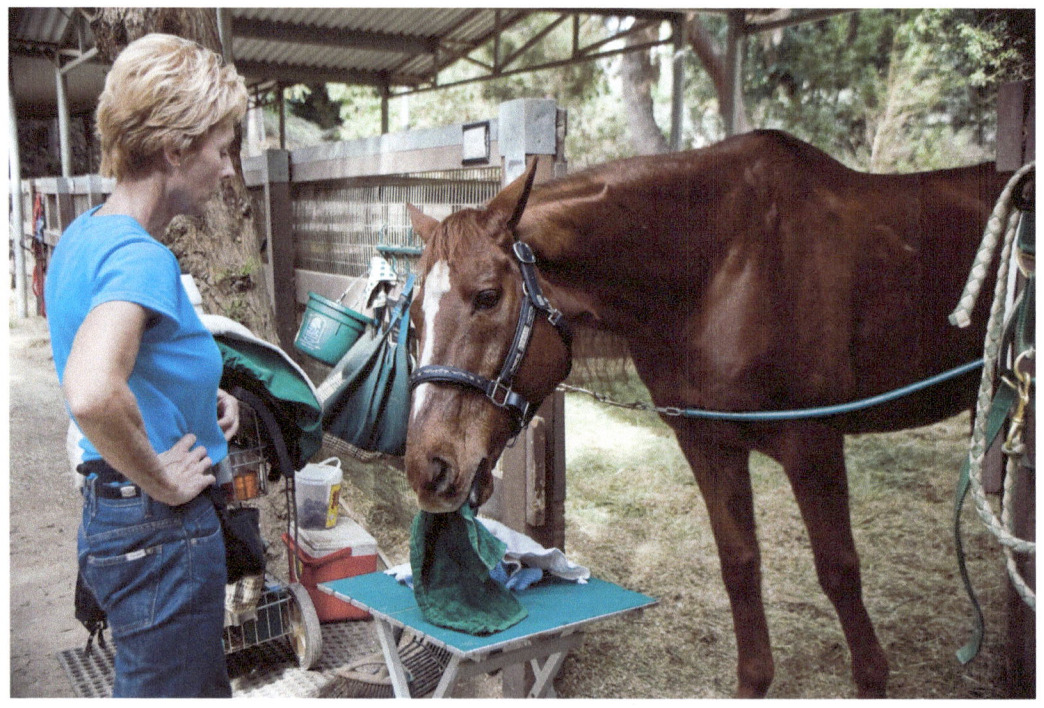

Playing With Lukas

Letters of the alphabet, bunches of them, in different sizes and colors. What if?, I thought. I had my husband, Doug, mount some black letters for me on light (for the color contrast) wood blocks and away we went. Not all was quick and easy, of course. I picked up the scattered letters and overturned desk as often as Lukas managed to find his letters in the beginning.

We were having a ball, and I paid no attention whatsoever to the disapproving glances. Increasingly, I heard, "Horses are not supposed to be able to do that." I turned a deaf ear. I'd already decided that Lukas would determine what and how I would teach him.

Towards the end of my stay at Brookside, I happened to pick up a book that would forever alter the course of our lives. *Beautiful Jim Key* by Mim Rivas is an incredibly moving and fascinating story about a horse, Beautiful Jim Key, who lived over one hundred years ago. Mim's saga describes a remarkable adventure of a horse and owner who changed not only the way animals are viewed, but were also a significant influence on civil rights. I had found our mentor. Apparently I wasn't the only oddball who thought horses were smart and deserved kindness and humane treatment.

Through the encouragement of friends, Lukas had his first video (of four) filmed during this time. I'd had so many people scoff in disbelief when I mentioned my smart horse that I wanted some type of reference for them. Meanwhile, the eventing trainers at Brookside had found it amusing to let the assistant's dog accost us, and Lukas, while laying down for me one day, was so startled that he got an eye full of dirt. A three hundred sixty-five dollar vet bill (that I paid) for flushing followed without an apology and another vicious dog encounter (while the two trainers watched and did nothing) led me to decide to move on. The Waltons, who had no idea what had been going on, were sincerely sorry and asked me to stay. I had felt the pull to return to nursing even prior to this and had already accepted a position near our new stables. We parted, promising to stay in touch.

Chapter 9   Reflection

*In every winter's heart lies a quivering spring,
and behind the veil of each night waits a smiling dawn.*

~ Kahlil Gibran

I chose our new stables (let's just call it number five) for several reasons: it was very clean, secure, and best of all, no trainers in sight. A small family owned and run operation, it had everything that Lukas and I would need for the next two years that we stayed. I spent this time enjoying Lukas, making up new games, and thinking: How much could he really understand? This was my first glimpse into a very different and self-assured Lukas that would soon burst out full force.

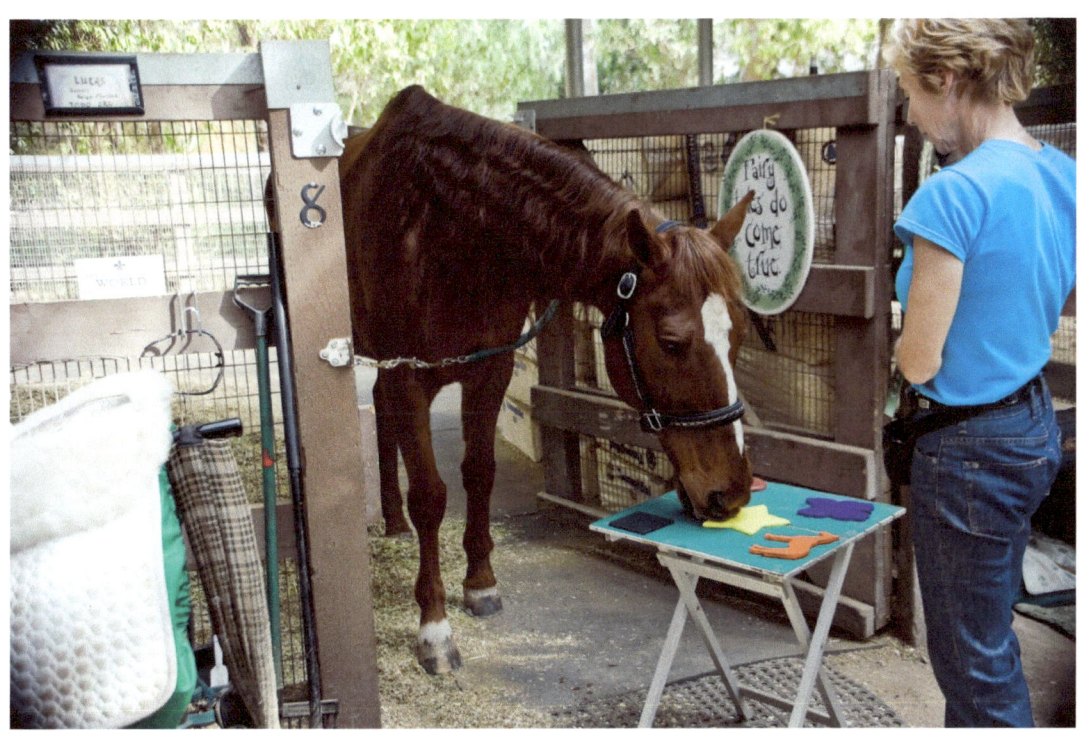

He quickly became the darling of the barn and the caretakers who lived there. He flourished with the attention he received, and I was glad to have a chance to confirm the lessons. By now we had added passage, fetching, catching, yes, crossing his front legs, putting all four legs together, acting lame, and shape and number discrimination.

Without any distractions or animosity towards us, we relaxed into a comfortable routine that gave us time to absorb and fine-tune his comprehension. This also began our concentrated probing into advanced concepts.

I'd already been experimenting with object permanence: I'd put his towel or my jacket somewhere and he'd look for it. We'd also worked with spatial relationships—Lukas being able to put something somewhere besides giving it to me. Did I set out to teach him all of these things?, I'm often asked. No, certainly not. I was just as surprised that he could learn these as others have been. The difference, I suppose, is my obstinance, determination, and love of horses. "Horses are not supposed to be able to do that," became a common and motivating topic. I'd become absolutely convinced that if people realized how intelligent and sentient horses were, they would then treat them better. This is what fueled my every move and decision. Not once have I ever considered this a burden or inconvenience—only a duty and honor.

My new job was at an adult day care center for chronic mentally ill patients. My work provided a rich and poignant affirmation for my beliefs and principles. Over one hundred participants a day would be transported in from the surrounding communities to have a brief, enjoyable respite from their often tragic and desperate lives. And the gratitude abounded! Such was the appreciation for the simplest, most basic items: a toothbrush, a spritz of perfume, or a little trinket brought from my home.

This time provided me with a daily reminder to contribute to my utmost and that Lukas and I needed to press on. I also had the tremendously rewarding experience during this period of training and including Wendel (my Cavalier) as a certified therapy dog for Hospice volunteering. In addition, I started bringing him with me to the Center and enjoyed countless hours of sharing a pet with animal lovers who could no longer take care of or afford the comfort of their presence.

As you've most likely concluded on your own by now, my message extends far beyond the stables. As part of this journey, my burning desire is that the practice of kindness towards all creatures grows. I now know, beyond a shadow of a doubt, that we are made kind by being kind.

Lukas continued to learn during this time. We included the rear, stay and come, and backward Spanish Walk. A serious bout of colic put things on hold, but he came back as eager as ever, if a bit thinner. His weight has been a constant concern of mine. His diet of timothy hay (free fed) and some alfalfa, along with multiple supplements, barely keep his attention, and I still, to this day, attempt to entice him to eat on a daily basis.

Once again, a matter of principles related to patient care prevented me from staying longer than a year and a half at the day care center, and I accepted a position as a case manager at a hospital in Pasadena. Little did I know at the time, that this seemingly typical (for me) decision would end up as the catalyst for transforming our lives.

Chapter 10   Renewal

I am not bound to win, but I am bound to be true.
I am not bound to succeed, but I am bound to live up to what light I have.

~ Abraham Lincoln

I soon found the drive from Pasadena to Lukas' stable exhausting. I was driving more than three hours a day in order to get to work and visit him afterwards. In the more than eight years I've had him, I've rarely missed a day seeing him. The one and only downside to all this has been his need for my attention on a daily basis. Within six months of purchasing him, he became increasingly ill when I was absent for more than two days.

Since that time, he's always had a nanny to monitor him if I wasn't able to make it out to see him. I've trained each of his nannies to just talk to him, brush him, and let him know I'm coming right back. They'll call me and put the phone to his ear so I can tell him to "Be good." And so it happened that the stable caretaker became Lukas' new nanny. Two to three days a week she would look after him—when I couldn't make it out—and call me with a report. This went well....for a while.

I don't permit other people to turn Lukas out (loose in an arena)—ever. His calmness with me belies a very mischievous and just under the surface volatility. That's my only rule—the danger is too great otherwise. He becomes easily frenzied and won't let others near him. I'd seen this in him several times in the past. One incident illustrated this perfectly. I'd arrived one day at Brookside, and the barn manager (an experienced horseman) approached me shaking his head saying, "The waterer broke in your stall, and Lukas wouldn't even let us touch him. I had to get all the guys, surround him, and in a big circle escort him to another stall." Because of this, I must be with him for all vet procedures, shoeing, and any necessary stall changes.

On this particular day, I drove up and immediately noticed Lukas was covered in dried sweat. My heart sank, already knowing what was coming. The nanny admitted that since he was so calm and sweet with her, she had let him loose in the arena the day before. According to bystanders, he ran wild for almost a half hour and was only caught with the help of four other people. After scouring his body, I took him out to check him—dead lame (limping). A vet call and hundreds of dollars in diagnostic testing (that I paid for) revealed only a muscle pull, thankfully. A momentary lapse in judgment by her, but the damage in me went deep. She and I had become dear friends and the disappointment was immense.

Arriving home, I glanced at the mail and in amazement noticed and opened another invitation from Linda and Keith Walton to return to Brookside. This time, it came with the assurance that the previous trainers had left. I was on the phone to Keith within minutes. Lukas would be on his way in the morning.

One of the most beautiful gifts on this wonderful journey has been meeting all our new friends. Lukas' hauler Chuck Erb and his wife Stacey, are among those. They've gone out of their way to help and accommodate us, and this time was no different. Lukas would be in an outside paddock twenty-four by thirty-six—plenty of fresh air and room and even a spot for his pedestal.

When we returned to Brookside in June 2009, I felt a resurgence of energy and drive like never before. The surroundings and atmosphere felt positively invigorating. Lukas and I surged ahead with new lessons that included proportion, same/different, and another that we're still working on—that of absentness (an advanced concept having to do with none). His eagerness and our bond deepened as we re-connected with the trails and each other.

In the hopes of helping horse rescues, I posted the training videos I had made of me and Lukas (each twenty-five minutes long; can you imagine?) on YouTube in July. Within weeks, his views were into the thousands, and I was starting to receive e-mails about him. Being new to computers at the time, I did my best to answer the increasing inquiries, sending out information to anyone who requested it so we could spread our message of kindness to animals, one click at a time.

Before I knew it, Lukas had a website and I was learning how to download. Doug suggested an early retirement for me to pursue my dream of helping horses, so I left nursing. The loveliest outcome so far has been the help and encouragement of strangers, now friends. What I thought I could never have or ask for in the past is now freely given to me for a shared noble purpose.

After several months, another serious bout of colic interrupted our studies, during which time I slept on the ground outside Lukas' stall. His brilliant vet, Dr. Vrono, performed above and beyond his duty to keep Lukas from going to the hospital, which would have been his doom due to his frail condition at the time and dependence on me. Lukas bounced back from this episode, was scoped (examined for ulcers) all clear, and we pushed on.

In October of 2009, I received a phone call from Bonnie Adams, the Southern California Director of CANTER, regarding Lukas becoming a Spokeshorse for the organization. The Communication Alliance To Network Thoroughbred Ex-Racehorses (CANTER) started as a solution to help racehorses find new careers by connecting buyers and sellers through posting racehorses for sale on the Internet.

Bonnie and I met, and I was immediately impressed with her dedication and energy. The following week, she called again to let me know she was bringing a friend with her on her next visit: Crystal Cruz of KMIR-NBC. Crystal's footage of me and Lukas playing (to back up Bonnie's powerful plea for intervention on behalf of racehorses) aired the following night, and we were told that Lukas' story spread like "wildfire" worldwide, which caught the attention of the Associated Press.

Lukas seemed to revel in the excitement and attention. Always a ham before, I began to notice more nickering when I brought out the camera. Prior to this, he'd been somewhat on the shy side with strangers. But the appearances and visitors have boosted his confidence to the point that he's now able to perform demonstrations in front of noisy crowds, and he permits children to touch him adoringly.

Nothing seems to bother him anymore. Well, except for one thing: Bonnie sent me a horse off the track to train for two months (Mr. B), and we put him across from Lukas thinking that Mr. B could watch and learn. Lukas stared at us non-stop in a way that said loud and clear, "Come back here with me!"

Lukas and I now spend our days in joyful, peaceful harmony listening to the birds and playing. We take turns initiating games and being close. Our time together is precious, and we find fresh delight in every moment.

And now, dear reader, we're back at the beginning of our story, the present. As I've sat here writing this book, hundreds of e-mails have piled up—and I will answer every one. It's been a privilege having you join us on our journey. Lukas and I hope you've been moved to share our story to inspire hope and happiness in yourself and others.

What I Have Learned

*The highest reward for our efforts
is not what we get for it but what we become by it.*

~ John Ruskin

Lukas has taught me more than I'll ever be able to teach him. A common remark I've heard often is, "Lukas should be so grateful for all you've done for him." Well, by now you're probably aware that I'm the one who's grateful for the gift of his presence. I'm most indebted for his lesson of patience. I've always been resolute, and I'm fortunate to have had the chance to dig deeper than I ever dreamed I would have to. Had I known the obstacles in front of us, I still would have stayed the course, so convinced was I that a cast-off could be redeemed—as I was.

Lukas has taught me that horses do indeed have some form of consciousness. I may never be able to prove it, but the way he acts certainly indicates it. The refrain, "Horses are not supposed to be able to do that" is now expanding people's perceptions of animal capabilities, emotional qualities, and ways to approach training. The stirrings of a universal shift in consciousness and mainstream concern for animal well-being suggests that we're fulfilling our purpose: sharing gentle kindness. I've had a deep reverence for nature all my life, and the sense of connectedness I feel with him, and through him from the multitude of supporters, gives credence to my belief that we're all linked with a common bond through our love of animals.

Marti McGinnis at the Equine Connection, a global online community for equine rescue and welfare, summed it up for me beautifully in this way: "The journey that Ms. Murdock has initiated with Lukas serves as an enlightening example of how an animal-human partnering can transform not just individual lives, but whole populations as their sphere of upbeat, gentle influence wraps around a world ready to hear about their changes."

Lukas exemplifies all the qualities I've worked so hard to cultivate (and continue to struggle with) in myself: resilience, forgiveness, joy, trust, and humor. He's an example of how I'm supposed to live—happily in the moment, enjoying nothing better than each other's company and the preciousness of our lives. Lastly, he's taught me the meaning of selfless love and devotion.

Interviews with Karen

Joan Ranquet, Pet Talk Live Radio, April 7, 2010

Joan: I'm your host Joan Ranquet. Today we have a special guest. We have is the World's Smartest Horse's personal trainer/owner Karen Murdock from California.

Karen: Hi, Joan. Thank you for having me on the show.

Joan: I want everyone to know that it's fun to Google the World's Smartest Horse because they'll find that right now it's Lukas. And Karen has written a great book called *Playing With Lukas* to tell her story. How old is Lukas now?

Karen: Lukas is seventeen now, Joan.

Joan: He's a seventeen-year-old thoroughbred and has been at the racetrack. Karen rescued him sort of. When we say somebody rescued somebody we think a lot of times that we rescue each other, would you agree?

Karen: Yes, very much so.

Joan: I would love for you to tell people about how you came to get Lukas and the beginning of your journey.

Karen: Thank you Joan, I'd be happy to. I first met Lukas out of a *Horse Trader* sale ad. He had been rescued out of a yard from the woman I purchased him from. She noticed him while she was driving by and felt so bad for him and took pity on him. He was skin and bones and his tail was a solid bat of dried mud. She took him home and reconditioned him intending to use him in her jumping string for amateur riders. But she said that after two years, he still just wasn't fitting in, so she put him up for sale. When I saw him I just fell in love with him and brought him home. At first, he didn't take well to competition training at the barn I had him at. He had some bad habits that surfaced. I managed to bring him back using trick training and behavior modification techniques.

Joan: It's amazing what you ended up doing with him. At the beginning, he just seemed to not be interested in competitions. But you were even challenged just to get him started riding, is that correct?

Karen: Yes, he was very resistant. I don't know if he was having flashbacks or this type of training regimen didn't suit him. He seemed to have his own style and his own opinion, and I just went with trick training and tried to figure out what he would most enjoy doing. That just took off to the point that I had trouble keeping up with him. He has an insatiable love of learning and a curiosity and desire to explore. This has been fantastically fun.

Joan: One of the things that intrigues me the most about the behavior modification you've done is that you know Lukas could have been in the throwaway category. And there are so many animals that end up in that category, would you agree?

Karen: That's true, Joan. Unfortunately, the nature of the economy makes it difficult to hold onto animals that don't show a lot of promise.

Joan: So when I look at what you did with Lukas as a horse, it's fascinating, because a lot of techniques you use could be done with dogs or even cats.

Karen: Yes, I've been a psychiatric nurse for twenty-five years. It's really helped me look at life, myself, others, and animals in a very different light, to enjoy each other in a reciprocal and interactive way. When you have that viewpoint, it changes everything about the way you relate to others and how they relate to you.

Joan: You have some YouTube videos that show the way you relate to Lukas. It's so calming and quite amazing. There's rewarding with food and praise and there's no frustration on your part if you get something wrong. It's more, I would almost say, continuum training.

Karen: That's right, I've trained all my dogs as well with these techniques. My spaniel, Wendel, and I do hospice pet therapy. This training is a way of interacting like when we were kids and we were at school and heard the recess bell; we could go play and enjoy and return to a simple basic way of being in the world that's joyful, playful, and happy.

Joan: It certainly looks happy! Can you tell listeners how to find your videos?

Karen: Oh, thank you Joan. It's www.youtube.com/profile/user. You type in PlayingWithLukas. You can also view them on the website at www.playingwithlukas.com.

Joan: And your book is called *Playing With Lukas*.

Karen: Yes we do a lot of playing. It seemed like a good title.

Joan: Where can people find your book?

Karen: It's at www.LuLu.com and it's available as an ebook or a print version and will also be carried by Amazon soon. Interestingly, we're associated with different therapy groups; the main one is HEAL (Humans and Equine Alliance for Learning) and they're located in Chehalis, Washington. They've been using Lukas' training model to help their trauma victims which has been a wonderful outreach, a great way of connecting with a lot of wonderful people.

Joan: That's amazing. How do your techniques end up helping some of the people?

Karen: They use the techniques to help the patients connect with the animals, to get in touch with their emotions, and to heal and grow through the traumatic events they've been through. The techniques I use have to do with shaping, a clicker-less type of training, and positive reinforcement. By combining all three of those, it's a powerful way of eliciting cooperation and things that students understand: how to relate and how to train. And it's good feedback for themselves on their gestures, their emotions, and the way they convey themselves in their messages.

Joan: Is it tempting to use these techniques in your work as a psychiatric nurse? Do you see an opening for the type of work you do in the psychiatric community?

Karen: Oh absolutely, Joan. I've used it on my patients for years. My husband and daughter swear I use it on them as well. Any time you have another's best interest at heart and it's not being used to impose your will on another, but only to help, that's going to most always be accepted and used in a positive way. It's a way in being gentle yet firm, setting limits, and guiding.

Joan: That's great. How long did it take you to figure out between the time you realized you weren't able to just hop on Lukas like a normal horse and ride him before you started using this approach?

Karen: Well, I always joke that it took me my whole life! Since I haven't needed to rush it and there wasn't any type of pressure, it was a gradual process that came about almost in an effortless way. From not having a sense of urgency or a need of anything for myself, but allowing him the time to understand and figure things out on his own. And as I look back, it now that actually seemed to speed things up. When you're in a hurry and want things done, that seems to take the longest time. Just having the leisure of enjoying and exploring, that in itself seemed to make the biggest difference.

Joan: It's certainly visible in the videos and evident throughout the book. I would love for you to tell people all the different things you do. Because listeners are so engaged with this show now, they'll have to wait to watch your YouTube videos.

Karen: You know what's so wonderful is what Lukas does is at liberty. It's done freely and without the use of any force. It's for people to see the joy and the eagerness that Lukas has. That's why I do the liberty training, and to show people you don't need to harm animals or force them. They're more than happy to go along, and now Lukas even initiates our games. He starts most of them. The list of what he can do is always being updated. Right now he smiles and moves his lips all over the place. Remember Mr. Ed? I watched Mr. Ed religiously as a kid and was so heartbroken when I found out that Mr. Ed couldn't actually move his lips like that. They had to use a fish line strung through the halter. I thought if Mr. Ed couldn't do it then, I'll have Lukas do it now. Lukas moves his lips all over the place, every which way. He'll pose to show people that he'll wait. He's not grabby for his treats—it's not the food he's after. He'll hold his pose in a frame and will nod yes and he squeaks a fuzzy toy for the kids. A big part of our mission is to include kids. So many kids nowadays don't have the opportunity to be around animals, especially large animals. That's why we do events like Pet Expo in Orange County.

Joan: Yes, I saw that. It looks like fun.

Karen: It's really to show the happy results of kind training, but also to expose kids to this. Many children have asked me if I would hold them so they could pet Lukas. That's the most amazingly fulfilling and wonderful experience. You know, I was amazed to read that the average child laughs over four hundred times/day versus the average adult who laughs less than five times. I think a lot of Lukas' appeal has to do with the fun we have and the joy we experience together. People have forgotten how to do that. I think we're really here to enjoy life, to treat each other well, and have fun. Not at the expense of others, but reciprocal play. And that's in essence why we started the tricks—and it just went from there.

Joan: I'd love to hear about the tricks.

Karen: Lukas does a dry and a wet kiss. For adults, he does dry and for the young at heart he gives them a big sloppy lick. He catches and yawns, he salutes, and he does pedestal work. And this is all at liberty—from verbal requests, body positioning, and gestures. He stays and comes. He'll goes out to a mark if I ask him and he stays at his mark. He does a three-legged pivot (a 180° rotation). He also does a curtsey, with two legs in front where he puts his head down between them. He bows, crosses his front legs, and puts his feet all together. He'll lay down and I sit on him. He does a passage which is a trot that's elevated and lofty—really spectacular. We play hide and seek a lot. Lukas has a towel that he tries to find for me if I put it in different places. He'll act lame, he pushes a cart, and he does a wonderful rear. He identifies shapes; he has different shapes he points to with his nose. He's able to discriminate colors by finding his green towel. I taught him proportion: bigger and smaller. I started with nine shapes and went to eight and one and seven and two and six and three. Now I'm at five and four. In addition, he's grasped the concept of same/ different. Most of this came about from my curiosity wondering how much he could learn. As wonderful and as exciting as my favorite tricks are, what I consider tricks are more like training. I don't think I've been able to tap even a small percentage of what's in there. It's fascinating to me what can be brought out. And it's not so much why would you do all of this; it's to make a point that if people realize how smart animals are, they would be less likely to harm them. And also to be nicer to each other.

Joan: And it gives everybody more value—it gives the animals more value, and it gives us more value for being able to tap into that energy. It seems a lot of what you do is some form of communication with Lukas. Have you ever thought in your mind something and he already does it before you even presented him with the task? I can tell from the videos that you guys have a telepathic thing going on.

Karen: Absolutely. Yes. You know, nowadays, with all the doom and gloom news, people are detached from nature. A lot of Lukas' mail is about people getting emotional when they see his videos or hear about our relationship. They let me know me it reminds them of how we're supposed to be and how we used to feel in relation to other creatures. That connection with nature is so important, and that's the big reason why we have such a problem in the world. We forget and we miss the simple, but important things.

Joan: And remembering the important things. It sort of expands out beyond the barn. But I want to remind people of the whole idea that Lukas could have been a throwaway horse because he was deemed unrideable or he was challenged when you first started riding him. There are a lot of horses like that. And even other animals, like dogs. When I looked at your book, I thought about how could you expand that into something that even dog people could do or even cat people. Is there a way you would play with dogs like that?

Karen: Of course. Wendel, my spaniel and I interact in that way. The techniques will transfer to any species—marine animals, cats, dogs, fish, birds—the techniques can definitely be used for any species including humans.

Joan: Wow many friends does Lukas have on Facebook now?

Karen: At last count, around five thousand. We had to make him a fan page.

Joan: Okay, well he has way more than me.

Karen: He seems to be the first horse since Mr. Ed that appeals to all breeds and disciplines: circus, barrel racers, dressage, jumping endurance riders. Even other species have joined the act! There's a shift and a readiness to view animals in a new light and accept different possibilities. With Lukas I expose people to a different way of thinking. I have kids write to me that they're trying different things with their animals and hopefully it will spread. It's an exciting time. I'm wondering how it's going to affect the future.

Joan: Well it sounds like you're affecting it in a positive way. I wanted to go back to something you mentioned before. What does it mean to be at liberty?

Karen: Liberty means that the horse is free and turned loose. I don't have any equipment. I don't have even own a whip, which is unusual in the horse world. What Lukas does is all free and of his own volition and eagerness.

Joan: That's great. You were also talking about dogs. What sorts of things do you do with dogs, like when you get them ready to work in hospice?

Karen: The training techniques are similar to what I do with Lukas: the shaping, the clickerless training, and the positive reinforcement. It's training them in small steps to move into larger, longer behavioral chains. My spaniel Wendel will stay, sit, come, lay down, wave, and do the Spanish walk. He has his own little pedestal. Whatever I ask he will happily do, and conversely, if I ask him to stay and just lay by the side of a hospice patient, to offer comfort, he's glad to do it.

Joan: There's a well known dressage training coach and she taught her dogs to Spanish walk. Are you putting together a new training video with your dogs?

Karen: That's in the works. We have so many requests and so much going on. But that's on our list. And anyone with questions can email me at the contact information on our website. Now, a lot of this information is included in the book, so that might help people get started.

Joan: I love that my dogs and cats engage and play together. I even love if the horses get involved. Sometimes at night we play silly games, and I'll put up a YouTube video of me jumping rope with my dogs and cats. Or I kick a ball for my dogs and watch the cats fly. I do what I can to be connected to them. Do you find that with your animals?

Karen: Definitely. A big part of my bond with Lukas is the way we interact and that's what most people are attracted to. The way we relate and mirror each other is like a reciprocal dance. Everything else fades away and it gives our minds a needed break from always wanting to achieve something or get somewhere or be someone. It's liberating and joyful to take breaks in our busy routines.

Joan: I enjoy reading books like *Alex & Me*. You also have a hero. Can you tell us who your hero is?

Karen: I would have to say Beautiful Jim Key. He's a horse that lived in the early 1900s and was trained by Dr. Key, a self-proclaimed doctor. Their story is a fascinating look at animal-human interactions and what can be accomplished with kindness. The doctor trained Jim to be the smartest horse that ever lived. His IQ was estimated to be the equivalent of a fifth grader. He made change, spelled long names, and travelled across the country with the doctor promoting kindness to animals, and also civil rights. Reading about Jim Key helped me teach Lukas some of the things he's learned. There may be a movie made about Jim as well as a documentary in the future.

Joan: I was reading your book, *Playing With Lukas*. One of the great things about it is it's more hands on for people wanting to connect on a deeper way with their animals, especially if they're having a challenge and need to find something that really works. Karen, thank you for joining us. It was great to have you on the show. We'll have to have you again when your training manual comes out. You can contact Karen and Lukas at www.PlayingWithLukas.com.

Karen: Thanks for having me, and I appreciate your sharing Lukas' story.

Pet Talk Live Radio; www.contacttalkradio.com/hosts/joan_ranquet.html

Caroline Putus, Confidence Club, February 18, 2010

Caroline: Karen, I'm so pleased to have you on this call. Karen is the owner and trainer of Lukas, the world's smartest horse. And he's gorgeous. Karen has loads of stuff to tell us that will help you and me with training our own horses. Karen, could tell us a little about your background with horses and how you developed your training methods?

Karen: I'd be glad to Caroline, and thank you so much for having me on the show. I started training animals when I was a young girl. I started with dogs and over the years became fascinated with the way animals learn. I've always loved horses. From an early age I read, watched, and talked to everybody I could contact. I watched videos from every type of training, from circus and barrel racing to dressage and show jumping. I also became interested in the way marine mammals are trained—dolphins, whales, and so forth. So I put a lot of different types of techniques together and came up with my own system. It's an extremely effective approach that blends shaping, clicker training, and positive reinforcement.

Caroline: It sounds absolutely amazing. And it's certainly something you were destined to do, because you were interested at such an early age.

Karen: Absolutely, Caroline, that has become our purpose—to share the happy results of kind training and show how wonderful and smart horses are, so hopefully people will treat them better. I've been a psychiatric nurse for the last twenty-five years, so I know firsthand that our emotions impact those around us and also our environment.

Caroline: Have you been influenced by other trainers?

Karen: Not really. I pulled bits and pieces from a variety of trainers over many years. Primarily it was things I didn't want to use with my horses—such as force or any type of restraining devices. I wanted to let the animals show me what they wanted to learn and how best to approach them.

Caroline: I think it's fascinating. I'd like to know how to apply some of your methods with my horse. How did you meet Lukas and what's his story?

Karen: I've always loved thoroughbreds, Caroline. I mostly enjoy the challenge—they're such sensitive and intelligent creatures. I'd just found a home for a mare

I'd been training and happened to pick up the local *Horse Trader*. I noticed Lukas' picture and went to take a look at him. I liked his demeanor and his attitude and went back to see him again and purchased him.

Caroline: And he's so beautiful as well, isn't he?

Karen: Yes, thank you. He's just as beautiful on the inside as the outside. He raced as a two-year-old; two races at Santa Anita and one at Del Mar under the name Just Ask Mike. He left the track after injuring his front tendons and then ended up changing hands several times over the next six years. The lady I bought him from had noticed him in a yard when she drove by. When she saw how neglected and emaciated he was, she offered to buy him out of pity. She tried to condition him for her amateur jumping program, but he wasn't fitting in so she put him up for sale. He'd been passed around so many times—what a way to live. I think that's part of our bond now; he's so grateful and willing to receive and return my love.

Caroline: Definitely. Was it difficult to train him and did you ever feel like giving up?

Karen: When I bought him, I was working full time at a difficult job. The hospital needed a lot of nursing help. So, I did something I'd never done before and I will never do again—I enlisted the help of a local trainer to get Lukas prepared for lower level competition. As it turned out, I don't know if it reminded of his past, but he completely snapped. He become sullen, disagreeable, resistant, and quite unmanageable. I had serious doubts about bringing him back, in fact I asked a friend if she could find a home for him because she knew a lot of people in the area. I thought he might be happier as a lawn ornament. My friend encouraged me to stick with it, and I did because I felt obligated and responsible. I was curious to see what could come up since I could see glimmers of his potential. He was at the point where it could have gone either way. My friend suggested I change his diet from alfalfa to timothy hay. That seemed to make a difference along with starting the clicker training and shaping. I'm so thankful I didn't give up.

Caroline: There was something there that made you stick with it.

Karen: There was something, and I think it was that I didn't realize at first how sensitive and reactive he was. I had the experience since I used to train horses professionally, but he made me reconsider all that I knew. In the past, I had salvaged auction horses and also started young horses, but Lukas required a whole new strategy. He was only the second horse I'd ever ridden that I had to grab by the mane to stay on several times. That's why I let his mane grow long, because he was so dangerous at first with his spinning rodeo bucking. For the first time in my life, I even lost a stirrup while riding.

Caroline: Before we go on, I wanted to mention that you've done a lot with Lukas and now a lot of people know about it. Where can people find out more about you and Lukas?

Karen: Thanks for asking. You can go to YouTube and see all of his wonderful videos. Just search for PlayingwithLukas. You can also visit Lukas' website at www.playingwithlukas.com. In addition, I just finished writing his book *Playing With Lukas*, due to popular demand. People have really wanted to know more about him. I've just received the latest edits from our great writing coach and copyeditor, Andrea Susan Glass of WritersWay. It will be available with a link from our website to www.LuLu.com.

Caroline: Will it be available on Amazon?

Karen: It will be there shortly.

Caroline: That sounds fantastic. What's the book about?

Karen: Well, I felt I had to write it, Caroline, because so many people wanted to know about our background and relationship and the training techniques. I've also been asked to write a training manual, so I'm working on that as well. Now Lukas is the spokes-horse for TROTT and the poster boy for the California Breeders Association. So it's all been about raising awareness. Our services have been to benefit non-profits.

Caroline: What you do is so different from the old-fashioned conventional ways we dealt with horses. What you're doing with Lukas has to be the future.

Karen: It's been a wonderful adventure and I think the best thing about it has been all the animal lovers who've converged on the story. People are ready for a change—to view animals and treat them in a different way. Horses have been thought to be dumb for so long, and in my opinion that's just the way they've been tested, in a constricted way that's not really conductive to learning. I'm hoping people will see that we all need to live with respect and appreciation for each other. It goes way beyond the barn.

Caroline: Can you give us some tips on how to incorporate fun and play into our everyday schedule with horses? People may think they need special facilities or equipment. And how much time do you need to do the training each day?

Karen: Those are excellent questions. I've been teased often that I'm never going to make any money from equipment because I don't use any at all in my training. Lukas is trained through liberty with patience and kindness. It's not the technique so much as the approach. If you have a respectful and appreciative approach, that's the main thing. The techniques can all be learned but they're not as important as your attitude and having a way of interacting with the horse in a playful manner. What Lukas and I do is very spontaneous and unplanned with no agenda. It's more of an interactive process that we enjoy, exploring and sharing with each other—a kind of blending of our spirits. It's a feeling more than any type of rules or guidelines.

Caroline: I think that's an important point, that you just want to be together and don't expect anything.

Karen: That's so true. And as far as the time, our sessions vary. I've never timed it because it's all dictated by the horse. As long as the horse is eager and willing and we're engaged, the session continues. Lukas will play now for hours; he's eager and wants to keep learning more. And you can do multiple brief sessions. With Lukas, it's usually every day for about three hours total from the time I arrive including grooming, walking, cleaning, and feeding. But during that time I don't waste a single second—it's all so precious. A lot of my training takes place in the stall. That's where I like to get the horse's attention and develop that sense of trust and confidence. I help the horse to associate my voice and whistles with positive outcomes. If Lukas gets nervous for any reason, I can use those my voice, whistling, or any of the tools I use to focus his attention back on me. Horses can't think of more than one thing at a time so by reminding him of my presence and that I'm his security, I can alleviate a lot of anxiety when he's out in public.

Caroline: So true. One of our listeners had a question about her horse not willing to go anywhere near plastic bags or plastic cones. She wants to desensitize him from this and incorporate it with fun training. What would you suggest?

Karen: Sure, Caroline. Well, when Lukas was at his worst, he would spook in his own stall. He was afraid and startled at just about everything. Here's how I got him over that: I would tie plastic to my shirt or to my lead rope in a safe way. You have to use good judgment and always maintain safety where spooking comes into play. You'll know that exact moment when you see the ears go up, the nostrils flair, and the body stiffens. As much as Lukas has learned from me, I've learned just as much from him. Be aware of your horse, and watch them when they start to work. That's when you back off and reintroduce, *before* they start to get worried. Tension is the enemy of progress. Learning can only take place when there's a bit of interest, otherwise there's no motivation. Lukas used to be ridiculous with plastic and cones. So I would put them in the stall near his feeder or have them on the ground and hang bags out of my pockets and make noises with them.

Bikes gave us a terrible time. So I borrowed one from the stable fellow and rode it back and forth frequently in front of the stall. Eventually, I took Lukas out and I rode the bike and led him following along. So my point is to introduce things in a non-confrontational way. When we went to our first big event, there were strollers, noisy bleachers, and we had to go through a vendors row with loud speakers and perform a demo in front of a large audience. Every sort of surprise you could imagine, but he never looked twice at a thing. Nothing in his training could have prepared him for what we faced. So it does work if you expose them gradually and carefully. Walk your horse out and lead him around and when the horse starts to notice things or begins to worry, you can sort of zig-zag or circle to get closer slowly and casually. It's teaching them to accept things—that it's all just a part of life.

Caroline: Wow! Great stuff, Karen. Here's another question. A listener wants to know how to teach his horse to lower her head when she gets stressed while being ridden.

Karen: The head lowering is a physiological relaxation response that results in the horse becoming calmer and easier to get along with. To do that is a shaping technique that's quite simple. Shaping just means you'll be using a cue and hoping to get some type of a response towards the desired behavior. I've found good success by resting my hand lightly on the horse's poll, right behind the ears. And when there's any type of downward movement at all, I release my hand and immediately say, "Good." If it's appropriate I'll use a treat of carrot slivers. The strategy of rewards is an entire book in itself. My book *Playing With Lukas* goes into that in greater detail. But what's important to remember is to use light pressure. Don't use any excess force. The signal should be momentary and become *less* as the horse's understanding improves. You can also incorporate a little flick of your left wrist to help the horse transfer the lesson to a non-tactile cue. I pair non-tactile cues (gestures, body position, etc.) with touching cues in order to fade the touching cues. I think it's a beautiful way to promote the horse's willingness and no force is needed. We don't need all the equipment people seem to think is necessary. By teaching the horse to lower his head, you can then incorporate it into your walks when the horse begins to get anxious.

Caroline: Can you explain a little more about your techniques?

Karen: I became fascinated with clicker training years ago because of the effectiveness and incredible results. The specialized clicker system I use increases learning a hundred fold and magnifies the positive outcomes. I replace a click with my voice or a short low whistle. I don't want to carry around anything or for there to be any delays whatsoever, because I found that instantaneous capturing of the exact moment is the most effective way to train. So as the horse lowers its head, immediately with that inclination, I tell the horse, "Good," release the light pressure, and then follow up with a treat (preferable while the head is still down). You must capture the precise moment, the exact maximum effort considering the learner's stage of training. Then as I stretch out the request, I'll treat for extra efforts to draw out more of an improvement, always raising the bar. If you continue to reward for only a minimum movement, the horse won't lower his head further. You always want to do less and get more.

Caroline: You make it sound very achievable, Karen. The next question is something quite common. Her horse spooks at things behind him. Sometimes there's nothing she can see there. He's taken off before, even on the road, but otherwise, he's quiet to ride. Do you have any suggestions to help her?

Karen: The spooking is a loss of attention or focus. As long as the horse is paying attention to you and looking to see where you are and what you're doing, that won't happen. When attention wanders or the rider gets distracted, that's when problems can happen. As long as you keep the horse's attention on you, that can eliminate a lot of potential problems. With spooking, I'll notice when the horse starts to become concerned. At that point I insert what I want. I'll do a circle or a shoulder-in, which are both great distractions. I'll whistle or hum or do something that will help the horse refocus on me.

Caroline: That's so interesting to hear you sum it up like that, Karen.

Karen: I think what happens is the same with our lives—we don't notice when things are going well. Then when something bad happens, we react. So my philosophy is that when things are going good, I reward. When they start to go off track, I notice that right away and bring them back. I don't wait until things become a crisis. It's a very proactive position; to determine what goes on and to make choices rather than be at the mercy of circumstances.

Caroline: Here's the next question. His mare is well behaved but she can be unresponsive to ride. She'll ignore his leg and sometimes leans on the bit and tanks along, going faster than he wants. At other times, she goes too slow! What can he do to train her either from the ground or in the saddle to listen to him more?

Karen: What I would suggest is liberty work. To me it's magical. Getting the horse to listen to you on the ground provides a solid foundation that will help you with all your training whether it be under saddle or routine care. Often, the horse is holding back because the rider has lost his balance. Or the horse and rider get frustrated with each other, then the horse speeds up. It also occurs when the rider isn't paying attention and doesn't notice when a horse subtly starts to be "unresponsive." I use a release signal for everything I do; without a "stop signal" the horse doesn't know when to quit, so they guess and quit early or keep going. So Lukas continues until I ask him to do something else.

Caroline: I have one more question for you. The caller has a new horse (she's had him for three months) and she doesn't feel like they've bonded. He seems to just tolerate her and doesn't seem to enjoy it if she makes a fuss over him. How can she get him to respond to her?

Karen: That's a common question, Caroline. The bonding takes place as a natural outcome of proper training and attitude. The relationship develops because you earn it; you have to work at it, develop it, and cultivate it. It's a special quality that happens when you have an attitude of respect and appreciation. And you can also use some of the techniques in my book. For instance, practice getting the horse's attention by hearing your voice and watching your movements. They will become focused on what you want and try to please you, and you can then build on that using games. In my system, it's important to have fun. When we don't demand something from the horse or require something for ourselves, that's when our bond with our horse will become closer.

Caroline: Yes I'm sure you're right. People sometimes think bonding should be instantaneous. But when the horse meets someone new, it's difficult for them—more with some people than others.

Karen: Yes, a major component is their instinct for safety and security. So by establishing that clearly in their minds, that will change how they view you. If they know they can trust you and are confident in your ability to keep them safe and secure, that will produce a solid basis for bonding.

Caroline: Karen, I'm so grateful to you for being on my show. It's wonderful to talk to you and a great privilege. We need to remind people about your book and your web address so they can see what you're up to.

Karen: Thank you so much for having me, Caroline. It's been an honor and I hope it's been of help to your listeners. Lukas has a fan page on Facebook: www.facebook.com/playwithlukas. His videos are on You Tube: www.youtube.com/playingwithlukas. The book can be purchased through our website at www.PlayingWithLukas.com or through www.LulLu.com.

www.enjoyriding.com

Rick Lamb, The Horse Show, February 5, 2010

I'm Rick Lamb and this is the Horse Show. Today I'm interviewing Karen Murdock whose horse Lukas has been dubbed the world's smartest horse by both Yahoo! and Google, based on the number of references to him on the Internet. I'm going to ask her to explain some of the things Lukas does and how she trains him. Lukas is a rescue horse off the track, a thoroughbred. We'll also make references to a historical horse named Beautiful Jim Key who lived about a hundred years ago. He was known as the world's smartest horse at the time. Karen has recreated some of the tricks that were done with that horse. I drew heavily upon the book about the Beautiful Jim Key by Mim E. Rivas in the TV episode we did about him.

Rick: I have live on our program Karen Murdock. We're going to talk about a remarkable horse you may have heard of called Lukas. Karen, welcome to the Horse Show.

Karen: Thank you Rick, so glad to be here.

Rick: Well, give us a quick synopsis of the wonderful things Lukas does, and then we'll get the back story after that, just to tenderize people.

Karen: Alright, sounds good. Lukas is the smartest horse in the world according to Yahoo! and Google rankings. He's been on ABC, CBS, NBC, CNN, HLN, Equisearch, Pet Live Radio, and the Associated Press released a feature story on him. He's been covered in most the major magazines, periodicals, and online sites. His claim to fame has been as a top liberty horse in the country. What I mean by that Rick is he performs free without any equipment whatsoever, not even a whip. In doing liberty, he performs the reverence (putting his head down between his extended front legs), the bow. He waves, smiles, catches, fetches, poses, nods yes, yawns, and he's able to do the Spanish walk, passage, and he stays, comes, and rears. But his real claim to fame, Rick, are his amazing abilities to count, spell, identify shapes, and discriminate colors. He's also been able to grasp the concepts of same/different, proportion (bigger and smaller), object permanence, and spatial relationships. In addition, I've been working with him on the concept of absence which is unheard of for horses.

Rick: You know I have a little bit of experience along these lines because we did a TV episode on Beautiful Jim Key and I know you're familiar with him. I heard that the author of the book on Jim, Mim E. Rivas, has contacted you. Is that true?

Karen: Yes, Rick. I'm thrilled that Mim and I have been in contact. She's also put us in touch with David Hoffman, the producer and writer of the movie that they're in the process getting funding for, and they've expressed interest in Lukas.

Rick: So had you known about Beautiful Jim Key before this?

Karen: Oh, absolutely. Jim is our hero as are Dr. Key's concepts of humane treatment for animals.

Rick: So did you set out to recreate some of Beautiful Jim Key's talents?

Karen: In a way, yes Rick, I did. That was part of our goal, and it was also a gradual process of exploration and allowing Lukas to keep going with it. It's been a wonderfully fun time.

Rick: I can imagine. I see the joy on your face when you talk about Lukas. And I know that with all the emails I get, that you're busy out there singing his praises and everybody is excited about it. Let's back up and get the back story. How did Lukas come into your life?

Karen: Well, I purchased Lukas as a nine-year-old green project horse. The gal I bought him from purchased him out of a yard when she saw him as she was driving by. She felt sorry for him and stopped to inquire about him. The owners said they had no horse owning experience and didn't even know what to feed him. She bought him in hopes of including him in her amateur jumping program. However, after almost two years, she found he was still not fitting in. She decided to sell him and advertised him in the *Horse Trader*; that's how I found him.

Rick: It doesn't sound like there was a lot to recommend him at the time you found him. What drew you to him?

Karen: I like to think there was more to this than coincidence; there's been one remarkable occurrence after another during all of this. I was attached to his look and his demeanor and the way he carried himself. He has the most thoughtful eyes and expression. I've been training animals for many years, so my background is such that he just really appealed to me and seemed challenging.

Rick: So do we know what breed he is?

Karen: Absolutely. He's a registered off-the-track thoroughbred. He raced in three races as a two-year old. He left the track as a two-year-old and changed hands over the course of the next six years. The previous owner bought him as an eight-year-old and kept him almost two years; he was almost ten when I got him.

Rick: Oh my gosh. There's a lot of tragic stories about horses that retire from the track. They're only taught to do one thing in the racing world, which is almost exactly the opposite of what they need to do on command when people are using them as recreational animals. So if you don't have someone who knows how to retrain them, they often have a very unhappy life. That sounds like what happened to him.

Karen: That's correct, Rick. It's so true. That's part of what our purpose has been in getting this information out there. We want to share Lukas with the world to show that there's hope for the second career racetrack horses. There's a lot of potential in this huge market we're overlooking. We don't need to go to Europe and spend fifty thousand dollars for a sport horse. We have a huge supply of wonderful horses here in the US that we can develop and use.

Rick: And those thoroughbreds, as a general rule, are fairly athletic horses. I know every horse is an individual, but these horses are bred to race so they must have some athletic ability.

Karen: That's true. I particularly chose a thoroughbred because they have a reputation for being somewhat flighty. I thought if I could turn around a nine-year-old spoiled, ruined, maxed out race horse, people would be less likely to do harm to their paints or quarter horses. If this can be done with Lukas—by a very ordinary older woman and an over-the-hill horse—if we can accomplish this, just imagine what young horses that are bred to do a real job can do and how they can succeed.

Rick: Did you set out with the goal in mind to make Lukas a trick horse, or were you just trying to make him a usable horse?

Karen: That's a good question, Rick. I really didn't have any preconceived goals. I wanted to find something we could share, enjoy, and do together—just the sheer joy of experiencing each other's company. And to show others what's possible.

Rick: What specifically do you want to show others?

Karen: One thing I like to do with Lukas is to expose children to farm animals. One gal I met while Lukas was in his display at the Equine Fair in Pomona, California, told me they had a cow on their property and a local child came to see it and thought it was a horse.

Rick: You and I grew up in a time where the first books we read had pictures of farm animals. I hear children's books are different now and they don't even teach kids about that stuff.

Karen: You're so right, Rick. Most kids nowadays are hooked up to iPods and iPhones. I didn't even have a cell phone until two years ago. I want to get kids to understand that animals have feelings and they're intelligent. We should learn to treat them better. I hope to share that message at Pet Expo in Orange County, California this April. What's happened is Lukas' website, which was only up for five months, has had over one million visits. People seem to be flocking to us. And it's not just the horse people, it's dog people, zoo people, bird people, etc. It's a wonderful time to be introducing Lukas and Beautiful Jim Key and Mim's book.

Rick: The story of Beautiful Jim Key is remarkable, but it happened in another time, so we don't know what's been lost in translation. We hear he was taught with kindness and was the World's Smartest Horse. But we can't verify any of this.

Karen: You make a good point in that it's just hearsay and second hand information. What's wonderful about sharing Lukas is that people can actually see the possibilities. The availability of video and the Internet makes it come alive and makes it easily accessible to anyone anywhere in the world.

Rick: About the same time as Jim Key, there was a German horse named Clever Hans owned by a school teacher. He was said to be this remarkable, intelligent horse capable of doing human-like problem solving. And they had experts testing him independently with the owner leaving the room. Once the owner was out of sight, the horse couldn't reproduce the same kinds of results. So what they concluded was that the owner was probably subconsciously or consciously cueing the horse, giving him something he was picking up on to give him the right answers. With Beautiful Jim Key coming along after that, there was a lot of skepticism so they did testing on Jim where they had Dr. Key leave the room and Jim was still able to perform. How are you answering skeptics about Lukas?

Karen: I can't dispute that Lukas may be picking up something from me. I don't know for sure. That's part of the magic and beauty of our relationship though, that he would even want to read what I'm attempting to transmit. The scientific community has also gotten curious. I've joined half a dozen groups and have been presenting papers and sending in information. It's all about sparking an interest and perhaps new research with different ways of looking at horse intelligence.

Rick: You're probably aware of Dr. Evelyn Hanggi who has done some research on horse behavior. Some of the ways you described Lukas' abilities made me think of some of her research: tests and determining things about color discrimination, size, and shape. Have you had a chance to meet her and talk to her about Lukas?

Karen: I have studied Dr. Hanggi's work and the Equine Research Foundation. What it looks like to me is that they do repetitive machine trials, and to her credit she's establishing a baseline for verifiable, recordable studies. That's important and it's what the scientific community requires. I would take it further and say that I think learning is better exemplified by a socially friendly context; similar to the way our children learn through interaction and reciprocal play.

Rick: So you don't really need to divorce the human element from the connection between the horse and the human since it's an integral part of the learning process?

Karen: For us it's crucial. I believe that's why Lukas does what he does for me. I'm not really inclined to do it another way.

Rick: Okay. Does anybody else handle Lukas or is this entirely you and Lukas? This is a very special animal to you, isn't he?

Karen: Yes, it's not that anyone else can't handle him. My husband, Doug, helps me a lot with him. But I prefer it to be an exclusive relationship. We're a team.

Rick: Karen, let me ask you one last question about the Beautiful Jim Key story. One fascinating element was that Dr. Key was with that horse from the moment it was born and around the clock until Dr. Key died. Dr. Key slept on a cot in the stall and they were always together. I wonder if there's a level of connection so profound when a horse and a human are in constant interaction.

Karen: Yes, definitely. It's a very intense connection between us. I see Lukas every single day without fail.

Rick: Have you ever slept on a cot in his stall?

Karen: Actually, I have when he's been ill. Our connection is so deep it can't even be described; you just have to see it. It becomes very clear as you watch his videos which are on YouTube and his website.

Rick: Do you have a certain training technique you use? I don't want you to share your proprietary secrets, but are you using the concepts of natural horsemanship or traditional animal training and reward and punishment, pressure and release?

Karen: I've been a psychiatric nurse for twenty-five years, and I've been obsessed with learning since I was a child. I studied birds, cats, marine mammals, and everything I could find about horses from circus to barrel racing to dressage. What it's boiled down to is behavior modification: I use shaping and a specialized version of clicker training along with positive reinforcement. Years ago, I became fascinated with the effectiveness of clicker training, however I felt it needed to be taken to a different level. So the system I came up with is a way to magnify the clicker training; it's like nothing I've seen and I've been training horses for thirty-seven years.

Rick: Is it on the rewards side?

Karen: It uses positive reinforcement. It's like the game we played as kids, Rick. Remember the hotter/colder game? By using an intermediate or in-between signal, this helps me lead the trainee to the desired behavior. It allows me to finish a training session, and then when I resume I can restart that same training lesson from where I left off. I don't have to keep going back to the beginning. Another added benefit is that we'll end up with the desired behavior as far as we can go, and then when the learner starts to waiver from it, I'll use markers to bring them back. It produces the most rapid, best retained, and incredible associations I've ever seen.

Rick: Let me see if I understand this: the concept of clicker training embraces operative conditioning where you reward things you want to see repeated and punish things you don't want to see repeated. It sounds like you found ways to give additional rewards along the way that say you're getting warmer, you're not there yet, but you're getting warmer. Ah, you're there. Big reward. So it's degrees of rewarding in a way.

Karen: Yes, and that potentiates the learning like you wouldn't believe. It's a way they learn to learn, and that's where his attention and his eagerness come from. Because it then becomes a game and interactive reciprocal way of playing. He's trying things constantly, and it's spontaneous exploration where I'm watching him and he's watching me like when we were kids.

Rick: Well this is fascinating from a number of standpoints. For one thing, any time we can get a horse to be curious, we know he's no longer fearful because those things are mutually exclusive in a horse's brain. If you get him exploring, which is a manifestation of curiosity, then he's not worried about his safety, which is good. That's the baseline you want to start at so he feels safe with you. And you've also tapped into a drive that some people call the play drive, where learning can be an enjoyable experience for the horse.

Karen: You made an excellent point about the fearfulness. He used to spook in his own stall. He was that unsafe and dangerous. The play drive you talk about replaces the fear-driven instinct behaviors, so it buffers that whole system. And the fun then over takes and creates a whole different realm to play in.

Rick: You're much different than I expected. You're very deep, and I offer that as a most sincere compliment.

Karen: Thank you, Rick.

Rick: It's been fascinating talking with Karen Murdock about her horse, the remarkable Lukas. He has his own website at www.playingwithlukas.com. Not many horses have their own website. Beautiful Jim Key didn't. Karen, any final words you want to leave with my audience?

Karen: Thank you so much Rick. I appreciate your time and interest in us. I appreciate the horse rescues and the CTBA. And Lukas' book is coming out soon.

Rick: He writes too?

Karen: I wish he could.

Rick: How would he hold the pen? Oh I know, he uses a computer!

Karen: Actually Lukas has a ghostwriter and she's keeping me on track. So we'll have a book out soon.

Rick: Fantastic! And let me know if the Beautiful Jim Key Movie gets made. Thanks, Karen.

Karen: Thank you, Rick.

www.thehorseshow.com

Press Releases

FOR IMMEDIATE RELEASE
FOR ADDITIONAL INFORMATION CONTACT:
Karen Murdock: info@playingwithlukas.com
http://www.playingwithlukas.com
(714) 403-7730

LUKAS' DOCUMENTARY TO BE RELEASED SOON
Dedicated To Hope And Happiness For All Creatures
The World's Smartest Horse Gets His Own Make-Up Artist!!

Walnut, California, June 28, 2010 - **Lukas,** The World's Smartest Horse according to **The World Records Academy**, has completed filming of his long awaited documentary. The touching story follows Lukas as a "race track reject" to becoming a well loved horse hero around the globe.

Produced by **Hadi Khalil** of **International Production and Advertising**, the documentary will include excerpts from Lukas' races at Santa Anita in 1995 (courtesy of HRTV) to his most recent appearance on **Inside Edition**. Guest interviews with **Dr. Don Scott Vrono**, **Dawn Mellen** (After The Finish Line), **Andrea Glass** (WritersWay), **Stacey Erb** (Chuck Erb Horse Transportation), and **Tat Yakutis** (Yakutis Enterprises) create a moving account of the former rescue's journey.

The purpose of the movie according to Karen Murdock, Lukas' owner/trainer, is "to convey a message that not fitting into a mold, or even failing, perhaps many times, doesn't mean we should give up on ourselves or others. It is still entirely possible to thrive and flourish, and best of all, to help others through difficulties, despite hardship."

The documentary showcases Lukas' extensive liberty repertoire: the bow, curtsy, laying down, fetch, catch, passage, Spanish Walk, stay and come, pose, pedestal, figure eights, yawn, smile, kiss, nod, feet together, jambette, wave, being blindfolded, and the rear. The spectacular footage also includes some previous cognitive task favorites such as spelling, counting, identifying shapes, and discriminating colors, along with his recent **Guinness record attempt**: "Most numbers identified by a horse in one minute."

Fascinating glimpses of newer games are also featured including proportion, same/different, spatial relationships, object permanence, and absentness. Murdock states, "This last concept, absentness, has long been thought to exist only in primates (monkeys, apes, and humans), and some parrots." Lukas clearly exhibits this comprehension. Laughs Murdock, "That may have to be another Guinness record attempt!"

###

FOR IMMEDIATE RELEASE
FOR ADDITIONAL INFORMATION CONTACT:
Karen Murdock: info@playingwithlukas.com
http://www.playingwithlukas.com
(714) 403-7730

PLAYING WITH LUKAS BOOK RELEASE
World's Smartest Horse Book Available Now

Walnut, California, March 8, 2010 - Due to popular demand, **Playing With Lukas** is available immediately as an e-book or a print version. The "Million Hit Horse" had so much interest in his story that owner/trainer Karen Murdock decided to release **Playing With Lukas** earlier than the original planned Spring date, based on Lukas' world-wide attention. "What's so amazing about all of this has been the mainstream appeal and wide-spread interest in a very touching and charming journey," according to Murdock. Lukas, an ex-racer, has attracted global acclaim for his liberty moves, cognitive abilities, and the bond that he and Murdock share.

Comparisons of Lukas to *Beautiful Jim Key*, the smartest horse ever to have lived, abound. Lukas is currently honored on both Yahoo! and Google with the title of "World's Smartest Horse" (living) with over seventy-four thousand references to him on Google alone. The popular Thoroughbred has many media friends who have made him an Internet sensation over the last six months. Kim Miller of *Riding Magazine* wrote, "Lukas is a poster boy for the potential of all horses, especially those facing bleak circumstances." "People used to say that Thoroughbreds were too 'flighty' to train," wrote Esther Marr of *The Blood Horse Magazine.* "With a world-renowned trickster named Lukas to prove them wrong, who would dare say that again?" "Karen Murdock is proud of her horse and the tricks he's learned, all at liberty and without a whip in sight," said Lisa Kemp at the *Equine Chronicle*. "She hopes that his accomplishments can inspire other success stories. It's amazing what you can do with training methods based on kindness, patience, and a foundation of positive reinforcement."

Murdock's system has the advantage of incorporating and complementing two major areas of learning: that which the animal does on his own and that which we can produce. By combining two teaching styles—clicker training and shaping—the effectiveness of the schooling is magnified tremendously. The former refrain "Horses are not supposed to be able to do that" is now expanding people's perceptions of animal capabilities and emotional qualities and new ways to approach training.

A fascinating glimpse into the world of horse intelligence and behavior combined with the triumph of overcoming extreme hardships makes **Playing With Lukas** one of the most important contributions to the study of horse training and horse-human interactions available.

The book is available at www.PlayingWithLukas.com as an e-book, and will be released in the spring as a print book at Amazon.com.

###

FOR IMMEDIATE RELEASE
FOR ADDITIONAL INFORMATION CONTACT:
Karen Murdock: info@playingwithlukas.com
http://www.playingwithlukas.com
(714) 403-7730

LUKAS ON THE ROAD FOR 2010 APPEARANCES

Walnut, Calif., January 21,2010 - LUKAS, and owner/trainer Karen Murdock, will be on the road again, (following the great HITS Horse Show in Thermal on January 31), thanks to master hauler **Chuck Erb**. This time they're headed to the Equine Affaire at the Pomona Fairplex February 4 - 7. Lukas is teaming up with his partners**, The California Thoroughbred Breeders Association** and **TROTT** (Training Racehorses Off The Track) to share the happy results of kind training (all proceeds and services are donated to help horses). Additional invitations include The International Equestrian Festival, The Western States Horse Expo and America's Family Pet Expo.

Rosemary Neeb, Director of the CTBA, has some great projects in the works, one of which is an extraordinary web documentary (funded by Oak Tree Racing Foundation and filmed by Yakutis Enterprises), that includes Lukas and an interview with Murdock. **Christy Chapman**, coordinator deluxe, will be busy with upcoming newsletters featuring the latest updates.

TROTT Director, **Bonnie Adams**, is getting the new organization off to a wonderful start for 2010 with a new training barn contract, wine tastings and a silent auction to benefit horses most urgently in need.

Neeb and Adams are true visionaries making a real difference in the lives of horses, with Chapman keeping everything in order. As for Murdock and Lukas, they will be packing!

We would love to meet you all; you're welcome to stop by and visit us in the Breed Pavilion where you can feel free to network and enjoy each other's (and Lukas') company.

###

FOR IMMEDIATE RELEASE
FOR ADDITIONAL INFORMATION CONTACT:
Karen Murdock: info@playingwithlukas.com
http://www.playingwithlukas.com
(714) 403-7730

LUKAS - ONE MILLION WEBSITE VISITS AND FIVE THOUSAND FACEBOOK FRIENDS IN FIVE MONTHS!!!

Walnut, Ca., January 7, 2010 - Lukas (owned and trained by Karen Murdock), who has attracted global attention for his phenomenal liberty tricks and movements, as well as scientific notice for his amazing abilities to spell, count, identify shapes and discriminate colors, has reached new heights.

In less than five months, the sixteen-year-old rescued off-the-track gelding has over five thousand Facebook friends, and his website had over ONE MILLION visits. A new Fan Page has been created for him by his web designer. According to the designer, "In all my years of designing websites, we've never seen anything like it! It reflects a genuine universal appeal of the bond between Karen and Lukas—love, devotion, kindness and fun all rolled into one place."

Murdock, who is more than slightly tech-challenged, is grateful for having the help to promote Lukas online. "It's wonderful that so many people have had the opportunity to see the happy results of kind training, thanks to our online exposure."

"The World's Smartest Horse" (according to Yahoo! and Google) is taking it all in stride. Lukas is preparing for his upcoming appearances at the HITS Desert Show Circuit in Thermal (Jan. 31), and the Equine Affaire (Feb. 4 to 7), to support his partners The California Thoroughbred Breeders Association and TROTT. Lukas will also be joined by Cindy Langlois, of *Riding Magazine* fame and long-time Lukas friend, who will autograph the current R.M. issue for the first fifty visitors.

FOR IMMEDIATE RELEASE
FOR ADDITIONAL INFORMATION CONTACT:
Karen Murdock: info@playingwithlukas.com
http://www.playingwithlukas.com
(714) 403-7730

LUKAS - THE WORLD'S SMARTEST HORSE TEAMS UP WITH CANTER AND THE C.T.B.A

Walnut, Ca., December 28, 2009 - Lukas, the World's Smartest Horse (according to Yahoo! and Google), and owner/trainer Karen Murdock, have teamed up with Canter (the Communication Alliance to Network Thoroughbred Ex-Racehorses) and The California Thoroughbred Breeder's Association to promote horse welfare awareness and responsible horse ownership. Lukas caused a media sensation when his original YouTube videos were posted on the Internet and he has since gone on to appear on NBC; CBS; ABC; CNN; HLN; and Equisearch. The Associated Press also recently released a feature story on him, and he has been in dozens of newspapers; blogs; newsletters and magazine articles. He is scheduled to appear at many upcoming events including the Grand Prix HITS Desert Circuit and The Equine Affaire.

Lukas' touching journey from an ex-racehorse, to a pitiable and neglected state in a back yard, fortunately rescued, and then purchased by Murdock has attracted world-wide attention and growing popularity. The sixteen-year-old Thoroughbred gelding and Murdock have been together for seven years, and his phenomenal liberty movements and tricks, combined with his abilities to spell, count, identify shapes and discriminate colors have also made him a strong presence on Facebook with many supportive horse loving friends.

It was very natural that Lukas' story would appeal to Bonnie Adams, the new Southern California Canter Director, and Rosemary Neeb, the Director of the California Thoroughbred Breeders Association—both life-long horse enthusiasts. "I am very honored to be associated with them. It's a privilege to be involved with their efforts," Murdock states. (All of her services and proceeds go to benefit the horses).

About Karen Murdock
Murdock has been fixing problem horses for over thirty years using a combination of shaping techniques, a specialized version of clicker training, and positive reinforcement. Her unique approach uses games and fun as a way to connect and bond with horses to build confidence, increase focus, and improve performance as well as develop willingness and trust. She is dedicated to sharing the happy results of kind training and is available for consultations.

The AHP Newsgroup is a benefit of membership and provides members with press releases and newsworthy items. On approval, submissions are sent from the AHP administrative office to the AHP-LIST of AHP member e-mail addresses. Submissions must contain information about an AHP member. Messages should be sent as text only in an e-mail message to ahorsepubs@aol.com. Attached files, such as PDF and images, will not be used. Messages may contain links, but please use the www or http:// that precedes the URL address. Images, logos or attached files will not be included or distributed. Members are urged to include contact information on image availability. Members are limited to two press releases per month. These news releases are also listed online at www.americanhorsepubs.org under AHP Newsgroup for easy reference. AHP has not verified the factual statements in any message and AHP assumes no responsibility for the contents of, or any damage resulting from, any communication in the Newsgroup. Publication in the Newsgroup is not an endorsement by the organization of any product, person, or policy. Members may unsubscribe to the AHP Newsgroup at any time by sending an e-mail message to Chris at ahorsepubs@aol.com requesting to remove your e-mail address from the list. By doing this you will remove your name from receiving all future messages sent to the AHP-LIST until you contact us to re-subscribe.

Frequently Asked Questions

1. How old is Lukas? He's seventeen as of 2010.

2. How long have you had him? Eight years.

3. What is his breeding? Lukas is a registered Thoroughbred by Crystal Water out of Paula Revere.

4. Did he race? Yes, he raced twice at Santa Anita and once at Del Mar.

5. How tall is he? 16.2 hands.

6. What is your favorite thing he does? Nickering.

7. Is he for sale? No way!

8. How long did it take you to teach all that? My whole lifetime.

9. Can other horses be like Lukas? I believe so, with the right person. I don't think he's all that different or special. What's special is the way we interact.

10. Are you going to train another horse? Time will tell, but for now I believe my most important role is sharing Lukas.

11. How do you feel about being famous? That's a funny question, because when I do get noticed or receive any attention, it's usually something along the lines of, "I know you! You're Lukas' Mom" and I leave it at that. I view any notoriety as a benefit to the horses and not any kind of goal for myself. Not needing anything other than that gives me a light-heartedness, which is liberating and energizing.

12. What's next? I'm becoming involved with the scientific community to share my findings and encourage more (and humane) animal research into animal intelligence and behavior. Also, I've been asked to put together a training manual that's very specific and detailed to help people on a step-by-step basis that we may combine with a video demonstrating my techniques.

In addition, we just attempted a Guinness World Record for "Most numbers identified by a horse in one minute" and we're waiting for the results of that. We've also just finished filming Lukas' documentary produced by International Production and Advertising. It features some wonderful new footage and interviews with a variety of guests. Furthermore, I plan on conducting clinics and attending conferences in order to help people enjoy their horses in a more fun and interactive way. And of course, continue playing with Lukas every chance I get

13. How would you describe your relationship with Lukas? Love beyond words.

Acknowledgments

Afoot and light-hearted I take to the open road,
Healthy, free, the world before me,
The long brown path leading wherever I choose.

~ Walt Whitman

I must first thank my ever supportive and encouraging family: husband Doug, daughter Angela, and brother Ernie. They may not have always understood all that I've hoped to accomplish, however, they knew how important it was to me and gave me their unending help and comfort. Words alone will never be enough to express my deepest gratitude for Doug's enduring respect for my life work and destiny.

This book has most certainly been a collaborative effort, and so many good-hearted people have converged on Lukas' story. And that's what has become the most beautiful aspect of our journey.

I'm indebted to our exceptional editor and coach, Andrea Glass, without whom this book could never have happened. Mr. Hadi Khalil at International Production & Advertising created Lukas' spectacular website and extraordinary documentary. He generously gave many hours of his time to make our dreams a reality. Staci Jansma, our wonderful assistant, has managed to keep everything in order despite my being tech-challenged.

The graciousness of the Waltons will always be remembered. The Erbs—Stacey and Chuck—for their steadfast loyalty and support. Kris Van Blaricom, Lukas' nanny, and now close friend, deserves special mention for her care of Lukas and her encouraging words. Rosemary Neeb, a fascinating and insightful horsewoman, gave me regular guidance and perspective. Lastly, I would also like to express my appreciation to our Facebook friends who offer daily inspiration.

Resources

Lukas' Home Page: www.playingwithlukas.com

Lukas and Karen's e-mail: info@playingwithlukas.com

Lukas' YouTube Channel: www.youtube.com/playingwithlukas

Lukas' Facebook Fan Page: www.facebook.com/playwithlukas

Lukas' Twitter Page: www.twitter.com/playingwlukas

International Production & Advertising: www.tvipa.com

Andrea Glass, Ghostwriting/copyediting: www.WritersWay.com

Staci Jansma, Administration: www.StaciJansma.com

www.ingramcontent.com/pod-product-compliance
Lightning Source LLC
Chambersburg PA
CBHW041832300426
44111CB00002B/58